W9-BOL-430

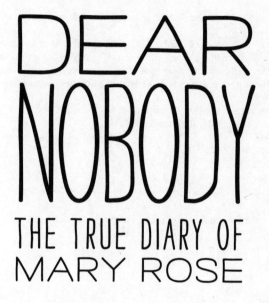

DEAR NOBODY

THE TRUE DIARY OF MARY ROSE

EDITED BY
GILLIAN McCAIN & LEGS McNEIL

ALL WORDS AND DRAWINGS BY
MARY ROSE

sourcebooks
fire

Published by Sourcebooks Fire, an imprint of Sourcebooks, Inc.
P.O. Box 4410, Naperville, Illinois 60567-4410
(630) 961-3900
Fax: (630) 961-2168
teenfire.sourcebooks.com

Library of Congress Cataloging-in-Publication data is on file with the publisher.

Printed and bound in the United States of America.
WOZ 10 9 8 7 6

Introduction

What if "Don't worry, you'll grow out of it" doesn't apply to you? How would you choose to live your teenage life knowing that any day could be your last?

Mary Rose wrote these journals between the ages of fifteen and seventeen. In them, she pours her heart out about everything from falling in love to fighting addiction to figuring out how to make her mark on the world. Her writing is powerful and raw—sometimes brutal, sometimes funny, and more often than not, insightful.

Though the Internet existed in in the mid-nineties, it was not yet accessible to everyone. Most high school kids still wrote by longhand, passed notes on paper, and called their friends on a landline. Parents couldn't track you via social media. If you were walking alone, at night, in the rain, along a desolate highway, you probably didn't have a cell phone to call for a ride home.

But most importantly in this case, you didn't chronicle your life in 140 characters or less. You wrote about your life in notebooks, described it in long letters to friends that you stamped and mailed, and took photographs that you got developed at the drugstore. You could probably count the number of friends you had on two hands. There was still a thing called privacy, and it was still possible to keep secrets about yourself. Your thoughts had room to develop. You had time to contemplate. You could describe, at length, what the water felt like when you went skinny-dipping that night. And you didn't have to worry that naked pictures would pop up on the Facebook the next day.

And yet the experiences and struggles that Mary Rose had are no different from the ones teenagers face today: loneliness, insecurity, depression, physical, emotional and sexual abuse, drug and alcohol problems, bullying, break-ups, and divorce.

Every word of this remarkable tale is true, though all of the names, except for Mary Roses's, have been changed to protect her anonymity. A friend of hers shared these journals with us after being asked, "What's the best thing that you have read lately?" Once we had the opportunity to read them ourselves, we were completely captivated. Though this book represents only a sample of the 600 pages of her work, we didn't change a word.

Welcome to Mary Rose's extraordinary world—we hope that you find her story as unforgettable as we do.

GILLIAN MCCAIN

READING, PA
LATE FALL, 1996

Dear Nobody,

Tonight I got arrested. I hate saying that, but it happens.

I had a 40 ounce beer in my hand and one in my book bag and I smelled like it. I was walking with my two friends, when this cop pulls up and goes, "Is something wrong?"

We all said nothing was wrong, but then the cop pointed to me and said, "Why does she look so sad?"

I made up some bullshit about how my boyfriend and I just broke up, but by then he had already seen the 40 ounce I was hiding in my coat.

They arrested me, but not my two friends, because they had no alcohol on them. My mom picked me up at the police station—and on the way back home we got into a fight over the time when I was twelve and she had pot in her car. A lot, too.

So I just got out of the car and tried to walk my drunken ass home, but it turns out I was walking in the wrong direction. I could've walked from Reading to Pottstown; that's over twenty miles. Shit, I bet I would've kept walking, if I hadn't seen this mall I knew, and was like, "Oh shit, what now?" I turned around and went to a store I saw closing up. It was after ten. Actually, I had been making pretty good time. I'm glad that I'm in fairly good shape right now, because I would never have made it if I was sick.

So I had time to think things through.

When I got back to Reading, I let this cop car see me, because it was past curfew and I wanted a ride home. Also, I had a feeling I wouldn't get fined; I figured there was no

3

way, after all this shit—that anything else that fucked up could happen to me.

The cop came into my house and talked with my mom and me. He said he wanted me to grow up to be happy and healthy, and that he wanted me to introduce him to my kids some day, and that he wanted to see me live to grow old.

First off, I'll never have kids.

And secondly, I'll never get old.

It's hard to grow old when you're dead.

Dear Nobody,

Today my mother's boyfriend, Joe, started threatening my life—saying he'd slit my throat and break my neck—and that it would be worth the jail time. When my mother tried to protect me, he swore she'd be dead in the river with me. She stopped protesting after that—she's a TERRIBLE swimmer.

Then Joe started in with even more violent threats; trying to break us down, the worst way he knew how, like calling me "a half-dead motherfucker!" When he started to get REALLY violent, my mother ran upstairs to get her pot out of the house so we could call the police. I told him that I wasn't scared of him and to "get out of our house **now!**" That made him even angrier, because his threats and bullying were futile against me. I guess he felt powerless. When he went to grab me, my mother jumped in between us and told him to get away from me. He grabbed her arm—the same arm I heard snap when my stepfather, Darrell, broke it in front of me when I was eight. Then Joe jerked her towards him. His breath was heaving and his eyes were wide with anger. My defenseless and pathetically weak mother had that familiar fear on her face and was meekly trying to fend him off. Nothing in me snapped—nothing flashed before my eyes; I remained calm and neutral. SOMEONE had to.

I refuse to live amid anger or fear. I looked directly into his crazed eyes; stared point-blank into his rage, as I'm sure no other woman ever has, especially a teenager. I spoke calmly and said, "Get off of my mother! Nobody touches her like that! Nobody will hurt my mother, especially not you! You are woman-beating trash—go back to jail!!!" (Joe did time for assault and kidnapping, among other things).

He was stunned for a minute, just like Darrell had been when I told him (practically) the same thing. But Joe's shock didn't last long. His flood of anger returned quickly enough for him to hurl my mother into a door that had a full-length mirror on it. She fell forward, holding her arm in pain. He was yelling even louder now but I still wasn't scared—my pulse didn't even raise enough for me to break into a sweat.

He started to holler, **"ALL RIGHT, YEAH, NOW THAT I'VE GOT ALL OF YOU BITCHES UP HERE WE'RE GOING TO SEE SOME SHIT FLY! THE NEIGHBORS CAN'T CALL THE COPS NOW, BECAUSE THEY CAN'T HEAR YOU MOTHERFUCKERS!!!"**

He was pushing things out of the way to get to me. By that time, I was on the bed, climbing to the window and yelling for help at the top of my lungs, **"SOMEBODY CALL THE POLICE! HELP! HELP US! HELP MY MOM!"**

He grabbed me and said, "What the fuck do you think you're doing, you cunt?!"

That's when he pinned me down on the bed and pulled my right arm back. My mother jumped up and grabbed him, and when he pushed her off, I had time to squirm away. Then my mother snatched the bag of pot—and we ran downstairs and out of our own house—for the hundredth time—while I screamed for help.

When we got to the car, I looked around. None of our

neighbors were looking out their windows. They just hid inside the paper-thin, poorly-insulated condos we all lived in.

Joe had said if we left him, he would call the cops and tell them mom had an ounce of weed on her. So I told my mother to give me the drugs, so if he did call the cops, I'd say it was mine. She handed it to me and I bent the bag so that it fit into my pocket. We left for my mom's friend's house—as we had done so many times before—only this time mom didn't mention what had happened with Joe—she just dropped off the pot and then we left.

My mom called Joe from payphones four times; getting more frustrated each time—because he wouldn't leave OUR house. He said he would only leave if she gave him $700. (Last time it was $280). As I watched my mother smoking nervously at the payphone, I got her checkbook and hid it under the seat of the car.

Mother. Mommy. Mom.

Phone in one hand, cigarette in the other—her eyes shifting uneasily and her voice trembling; the fluorescent light of the phone booth was forming a halo above her head. It reminded me of my childhood, when I envisioned my mother as a saint, as my angel, like most young children do, despite any circumstances. For a moment, I was saddened by the corruption of my childhood fallacies—but my level-headedness found me again when I overheard her offering to drive Joe home! I heard her say that she would pick him up and take him back to his parents house.

I jumped out of the car and screamed, **"YOU ARE NOT**

DRIVING HIM HOME! THERE'S NO WAY I WILL LET YOU BE ALONE IN A CAR WITH HIM FOR TWO HOURS!!!" (Joe had beaten her up in the car a few times before—he had tried to choke her to death; there had been bruises on her face and her throat). I started yelling and crying as we got back into the car. I kept telling her how scared I was for her, that she was the only parent I had left and that I couldn't bare to lose her. I begged, I pleaded, I ranted, I rationalized. I prayed. Then I got out of the car.

I took off walking in the opposite direction of our house. I had no idea where I was—or where I was going.

My mom didn't follow me at first—but pretty soon she pulled up next to me and told me to get in the car, unless I wanted to walk all the way home. After arguing with her for about ten minutes, I said, "If I get in the car, we have to drive right over to that payphone and you have to call the police. You have to show the cops the marks on your arms. Or we can stand here all night where at least I'll know you're safe."

A few seconds later my mother sped off, leaving me, her fifteen-year-old daughter, in the middle of an unfamiliar town—at midnight—afraid and alone. I sat down on a grassy hill near an intersection and cried. Then I walked back to the road and waited—half-hoping she'd be worried and come back for me.

<u>She never came back for me.</u>

It started to get cold. With the cold came drops of rain, so I looked for someplace to go. I found a bathroom with a broken door at a desolate gas station and went in there to cry

8

some more. After I was out of tears, and could only whimper, I started praying.

I asked God, "Why?"

Why did this happen?

Why did I feel so much pain?

I prayed some more—and then the rain stopped. I started walking towards the highway. It was so dark that I could only see where I was going when cars drove by, minutes apart from each other. The sounds from the woods nearby and the emptiness of the highway reminded me of something out of a horror film. Faces of missing girls from the 6 o'clock news passed through my mind. Instead of scaring myself, I decided to pray some more. I asked God to help me and my mother get home safely.

I walked for almost an hour, keeping my eyes open for my mother's car. I was walking as fast as I could without running. I tried to walk with my head up. Even though I was tired—I tried to walk proudly. I felt more like a soldier of God, than a child of God. By now I had seen and felt so much, that I knew God was there with me—helping me and loving me when no one else would.

I began to watch for a police car to pass by; knowing that even if they arrested me for being out after curfew, they'd at least give me an $80 ride home. (Or at the VERY least they'd give me directions.) Finally a van drove by and I could see the bill of a boy's hat silhouetted through the passenger windows. The van slowed down and stopped a few feet ahead. I slowed my walking, cautiously. I was ready to run just in case.

The boy in the hat popped his head out of the window and said, "Are you Megan?"

I shook my head and the woman driver asked where I was headed. I told her and she was kind enough to offer me a ride, even though her destination was in the complete opposite direction. She was being very friendly and so were the boys around my age who were sitting in the back. They asked me how old I was.

I said I was fifteen and one of the boys asked if I'd be going into 11th grade. Embarrassed, I told them that I'd be in 9th next year. I felt bad for not being completely honest, but I said it was because my family moved around so much. The lady seemed understanding, but the boys said nothing.

When I got home, it felt so good to be here, without that tyrant Joe. I ate what was supposed to be my dinner before we had to run out of the house. A movie came on HBO about a murderer that killed people in stalled cars on the highway. I tried not to watch it.

Mom got home safe—but looked sad. She said Joe was "moody" on the way home. That could have meant anything.

Well, that was my Wednesday.

Good night.

✗

Dear Nobody,

As if the thing with my mom's boyfriend, Joe, wasn't bad enough—my step-dad came by last night without even calling, asking for money. Darrell is my half-sister Nicole's biological dad; my step-dad—really. At least, I USED to think of him that way.

I hadn't seen Darrell this drunk and violent since mom was five months pregnant with Nicole and Darrell threw her on the bathroom floor. Then he threw me after her—then the phone—and then the phonebook, too. He told us we had a half hour to get the fuck out and never come back. I remember mom lying on her side—on the phone with her friend, Jane. She said that she thought her arm was broken, and that she couldn't walk. She had fresh bruises along her neck and arms—along with the old ones. I looked at what my HERO; my FATHER—had done. I was trembling—I could not even speak. I've never been so afraid in my entire life. I remembered how I had always wanted a father. Be careful what you wish for. That night ended like so many others; lying on Jane's cot—crying into a pillow. At least we were safe there.

My mom gave birth and nursed my baby sister with her broken arm. She had to work at a grocery store to make money. I'll never forget how sad and disappointing it all was—I had no daddy again, or dog. No house, not even an apartment. No friends, nothing of my own. I'll never forget it—and last night was no different.

⭐

Dear Nobody,

When I was little, I was so proud of Darrell—I even bragged about him sometimes. I called him Daddy. I really looked up to him. I even wanted to be a housepainter just like him—even AFTER he started to do drugs and beat my mom up.

After a while, I just got scared of him, but I still loved him a lot—for who he'd been BEFORE the drugs. People would come to the house when mom wasn't home and sell him cocaine. I saw it once. I was in the second grade and he was babysitting me and Nicole when this shitty little white car pulled up in the driveway, blaring rap music. Two fat black guys with gold chains got out and came into the kitchen. Nicole started crying.

Darrell gave them money and they gave him a plastic bag full of white powder. It was coke. One of the guys was sucking on a little pipe. I asked what was in the bag and Darrell sent me outside.

I saw my friend Crystal out back and I told her to look through our kitchen window. Crystal peered in and then asked why there were black people in my house. In Saginaw, the town we lived in then, there were no black people at all. It was a very small town; it didn't even have any stores. Crystal told me how she was scared of black people, but since I had to go into Philly a lot, I had met a lot of black people and they were all really nice. I told all this to Crystal, but we were both still really scared about WHY these guys were in my house.

While my stepdad and his "friends" were inside the kitchen,

I thought about the first time Darrell beat the shit out of me, when I was in first grade. It happened when I woke up one morning and walked into the living room. Darrell was sitting there watching TV, drinking a beer and eating a donut.

I hate donuts.

When I saw him there eating a donut (mom had bought a big box of them), I said to him, "You can have all the donuts."

Next thing I know he jumps up and starts screaming, "WHAT?! WHAT?"

Then he came after me—and hit me. Mom was still sleeping. It fucking hurt. I cried and cried, even after he was done. I tried to figure out why Darrell did that, and wondered if he thought I said, "You CAN'T have the rest of the donuts," like I was being a smart ass.

But then later, he came into my room, pulled me out of bed, sat me on his lap, handed me the donut he'd been eating and said, "Here. Eat that."

I guess that was Darrell's way of apologizing.

Dear Nobody,

I walked in the house and before I closed the door behind me, I got that feeling. I knew something was wrong. I could feel it in the air. My mother looked at me, and didn't speak. My heart began to race. I felt sickened. How could this be happening?

<u>We're moving away to the middle of nowhere—to Phoenixville!</u>

Mom wants to make a "fresh" start. Thanks, mom.

PHOENIXVILLE, PA
WINTER, 1997

Dear Nobody,

Ever since we moved here, I feel like I've got nothing any-more. It's such a small town that friendships here have been established years ago, and there's no room for even one more.

Sometimes I just get so bored of emotions. Sometimes I just get so bored of everything and I wonder if I'll ever be myself again. Maybe I just need a nap—or a new life. I've never been this lonely, and I know how it feels to be lonesome. Being a teenager, being alive, is hard enough—but I am lost. It's like I'm in a new world, a foreign country, all by myself—and I've got to construct a new life.

When you know nobody, and nobody knows you, it's impossible to make friends by accident. I try to tag along discreetly, and aloof, but I end up seeming like the tag along I am: **"Who's that girl? Why does she keep following us around?"** I follow people, hoping for affection, acceptance—a home. From clique to clique, group to group, I follow, only to be kicked aside—and at the end of the day, I am always left alone, droopy-eyed, and miserable—like a lonely, unloved puppy with its tail between its legs, and misery in its heart. I can only hope, and keep inviting myself along, keep following the group, hoping they won't mind.

HA—I used to be a leader—the center of my group of sub-jects, and now I've been banished to an unfamiliar kingdom.

Two months ago I'd have NEVER been a tag along! And now I consider myself lucky if there's anybody around to tag along with.

☆

Dear Nobody,

Lately, I'm having trouble remembering what it was like to have people around that are not so different from myself. The weekend is coming up. Hopefully it'll be okay. If even one guy calls me, or one decent girl wants to hang out, it'll be a good weekend.

I hate this. I'm obsessing over my loneliness. I dream about friendship—using the faces of strangers and laughs of unfamiliar voices.

I feel like a real life loser—and the game is life. I'm failing everywhere—academically, emotionally, socially, and even intellectually. I am losing myself on a bet. A bet that I can survive, that I can still be what destiny wants me to be. That soon my "losing streak" will end, that someday I'll get inspired, that someday I'll find God's gifts.

For now, I've got no choice but to get by on my dreams; and hope at least one of them becomes reality's beauties.

★

Dear Nobody,

A few nights ago Joe came here from Reading on some job. He brought with him two very attractive guys in my age range. They were both very polite and pleasant. We got drunk and smoked some weed. One of the guys was VERY cute, and the other was talkative and cute—but the quieter one was my favorite. He and I talked, and it ALMOST made me feel human again. I'm not sure how fucked up he was, but I was pretty blasted. He was dancing, and he tried to get me to dance. I guess I wasn't fucked up enough—or maybe I just liked watching him dance more?

Grrrrr—he was the nicest looking guy I'd seen for a while.

I was too fucked up to remember what we talked about, and I can barely remember them leaving.

I woke up early the next morning, knowing that today was a new day, with new nameless faces.

☆

Dear Nobody,

I feel sick, like I have the flu or something. I've got fevers, pains, headaches, sore throat, no appetite, vertigo, exhaustion and I can't breathe. I can't even cough to try and clear my lungs. My Tylenol with Codeine is barely helping, even if I take tablespoons instead of the usual teaspoons.

I really hate sickness.

If one thing in the world could be erased, I'd pick sickness. Then all the money spent on research and healthcare could be used to cure hunger and poverty. After that, it could be used by organizations that would help animals and women, children, or the defenseless. After that, it could be spent on improving the educational system. (And whatever is left over could be used for space exploration).

☆

Dear Nobody,

I was admitted into the hospital with a lung infection. They found a virus in my lungs similar to TB (tuberculosis). The doctor said that my immune system was "in the wrong gear" and attacking my hips. So this obstruction in between my hip socket and hip bone was slowly pushing apart those bones. I lay in bed at the hospital for over a week with traction strapped to my hip.

When I was first admitted, the doctors pulled down my pants and underwear—and stuck a four inch needle straight into my hip socket without any Novocain. It hurt like hell; and I was SO humiliated.

Later, the doctors told my mom that if she had waited any longer to bring me in—that my hip may never have healed. I would either not be able to walk, or have a terrible limp my whole life. They said they didn't know how much damage had already been done.

☆

Dear Nobody,

I'm getting out of the hospital today. I'm not getting much better, but my condition has stabilized. I don't care either way; I just want to be home. Before I left, the doctor lectured me on everything, including an awful conversation about "safe sex."

AS IF I DIDN'T ALREADY KNOW!

☆

Dear Nobody,

After leaving the hospital, I was confined to a wheelchair. Most of the girls at school were nice to me, and suddenly became my friend, out of pity. I would rather they just ignore me, than feel like someone's charity case. The boys at school were still horrible. It wasn't before long that I cried more from someone teasing me, than from my bones being slowly ripped apart.

Yesterday, I had just gone to lunch and was pushing along in my wheelchair, when some boys started making fun of me. They were being so cruel. I just sat there, on the verge of tears, and got so angry and so sick of everyone and all of my humiliation and torment that my shame turned into fury and rage and hatred. For them and for myself.

I looked at all of them—and screamed as loud as I could: **"Shut up, SHUT UP, SHUT UP, SHUT UP!!!"**

They all burst out laughing, like it was the funniest thing they'd ever heard. The little ugly, crippled girl was crying. One boy got right into my face and said, between laughs, "What are you gonna do? You can't even stand up!"

I felt my face growing hot and my body filling with adrenaline. I gripped the side of my wheelchair with my hands and stood up, screaming, **"I'm standing now assholes! I'm standing now!"** My legs were in so much pain that I could barely talk, but I didn't care—I didn't care that everyone was staring at me and laughing. I didn't care that it was hard to breathe. I didn't care that if I fell I could seriously hurt myself. I pushed myself forward and took a few steps. It felt like two

23

metal bars were being pushed into my hips. The pain became too much, and I fell back into the wheelchair, sobbing.

The boys who had been teasing me looked like they'd seen a ghost.

Hot tears were running down my cheeks, but I was proud of myself. I felt like I had taken back a little piece of the dignity that the wheelchair, the hospital, and the other kids had stolen from me.

The boys told everyone what I had done, about getting up like that. And I thought for a minute that everything would be okay. It wasn't. Then everyone started calling me a faker. They said I was pretending to be unable to walk for sympathy.

Later that day, I started crying in the middle of biology class—and had to be carried out of class in the teacher's arms. They took me through the hallway into the nurse's office. My mom came and got me. I haven't been back to school since.

Dear Nobody,

I HATE PEOPLE! At this point, almost everyone can just violently die, and I would sit back and laugh and say, **"MAY THEY BURN IN HELL!"**

I should have been born with a dick so the world could suck it.

I want to grow eight hundred feet tall and scream, **"FUCK YOU!"** so that the whole damn world hears it. Then I'll cut off everyone's middle finger and make 'em shove it up their asses—that way, even deaf people will get my point.

★

Dear Nobody,

Today I found a ring I'd lost some place years ago.

The ring is supposed to look gold, but the paint on it is peeled and tarnished. There's a small pink diamond on it, and a little, tarnished, golden-ballerina that loosely hangs from the diamond. It used to be worn on my ring finger, but now it only fits on my pinky. My mother bought it for me when I was nine, because I had just started dance lessons. The class was fun and I always looked forward to going to it twice a week. My dance instructor said I was really good. I made some new friends. And I didn't even mind having to do exercises before we started dancing.

At home I would dance, almost all the time—sometimes all night, until I had to go to bed. In our old house the basement was set up as my playroom and I brought a tape player down there and would dance. I always got a lot of costumes for Christmas and I loved to dress up and smear-on globs of make-up all over my face and put on performances. I would beg my parents to come downstairs for my shows. Neighbors, friends and visitors—no one was safe. If you came to our house, you would be nagged, begged and tormented to watch one of my performances. And one performance was never enough. If I had already talked you into watching one, you'd end up seeing three. I'd try to get you to stay for the whole entire tape if I could.

At the beginning of my "performances" everyone would act very impressed; but after a few songs they'd start looking bored and would tell me that this was the last song they were staying for. Sometimes I would dress my friends up in costumes and have them dance with me. But I would get really bossy with them—and we'd usually end up stopping in the middle of a song—either because I was shouting at them for getting in my way—or for not moving out of my way fast enough!

I always pretended that the green wall that I faced was rows and rows of people—who all knew my name and adored me. Yeah, I was famous. I would announce myself before turning on the music using a fake voice. Sometimes I introduced myself with a make-believe name, but usually not. I LOVED it!

Then my mom got divorced and we moved into a small two bedroom apartment—and the only place I could dance was in the living room. My cartwheels shook the TV stand—and the neighbors downstairs complained about the noise I would make flipping around.

So that's when I signed-up for dance lessons again. And I was loving it—until I had to quit because of my condition. My immune system was doing some strange things—something that had to do with the salt in my body and the obstruction of my hip joint. It was one of the most devastating things that has ever happened to me. It was four years before I was allowed to dance again.

And now it's happening all over again.

PHOENIXVILLE, PA

SPRING, 1997

Dear Nobody,

After I finally got out of the wheelchair and started getting better—the weirdest thing happened: I started getting <u>bitter</u>. Sometimes, getting better can be rather depressing. It can be really confusing. People tell you so much bullshit when you're sick. They elevate you and make you feel like a saint. I can't really explain how it feels to be in everyone's prayers and good thoughts. How it feels to be some fundraiser or charity mascot—to be liked by people because I'm the sick girl. But as soon as you're better—the charities move on and your place on everyone's prayer list gets lower and lower, until you're off the list, completely.

☆

Dear Nobody,

Have you ever heard someone say, "I can get through anything as long as I've got my friends?" Well, could they get through NOT having any friends?

I am really having a problem living through this. I mean, I'm not in crisis or anything, but sometimes I feel close to it. I am so desperate, and can only hope it is not evident to the people I am trying to befriend. I mean, I've met some friendly enough people, but no one has "taken me under their wing" (so to speak). It'd be my dream come true if I met a really friendly girl that wanted me to hang out with her, or even just wanted my phone number. I mean, this must be the hundredth Friday I haven't had any plans.

Man, it never used to be like this. Are friends really that hard to come by? I mean, shit; anyone else who moved here would probably have friends by now. This keeps eating away at my self-esteem, and I feel like shit. And that only makes it harder to make friends. What am I supposed to be getting out of this experience?

I am a loser. A natural-born loser. Well, at least lately.

I need to stop obsessing over this. It's ruining me. Not my life—I don't have one.

☆

Dear Nobody,

Well, I'm still bored here. Oh, I'm a little more used to it, and I am starting to like the nature around here, but the people still seem so dull. All the kids here hang out at the rope swing, even though it's too cold to go swimming yet. The kids I meet there (that I'm interested in) don't seem very interested in me for long, or if they are, I guess they can't show it. There are some cute guys my age that like me, but they're really not all that great. I did really like this one guy, Jonathan, but maybe I came across too weirdly. We did PCP in his white truck, and he was talking to me, but my answers were few and far between (probably because I was SO HIGH). I did ask him if he wanted my number, but there was no pen. I offered to get one, but he was in a hurry to go.

At first I really liked his buddy, Zack. He seemed like more of an intellectual (pretty cute, too), but even when he was high he still barely spoke to me. And when he was leaving, he never said anything like, "hope to see you again sometime" or some shit like that—but then again, neither did Jonathan.

Maybe my good looks intimidate them.

I still crush a little for this Zack, but I really CRUSH on Jonathan now. But man, I'd be cool with ANYONE cute, or nice, and who liked me—but I'd really like it to be Jonathan. I hope it's nice out tomorrow so I might see him again.

♡

Dear Nobody,

Last night, I got FUCKED UP with my mom and Joe. I might have tried to call someone that I don't know very well, but don't remember it, so I don't care. I woke up with a horrible stomachache from drinking so much. Eventually I went to the rope swing, and saw Jonathan. We smoked a bowl and I tried to talk to him. He was polite, but seemed distant. In fact he was kind of rude to me—still, I'm hoping he'll be there tomorrow.

Zack was there alone today, like me. Maybe he gets really lonely, too. He had to leave right away, so I couldn't talk to him as much as I would have liked. I really hate this—mentally and subconsciously pleading for friendship or a companion. It's not at all flattering to my ego—which, by the way, would have rejected even the CONCEPT of kissing ass for friends a few months ago. Zack left without saying goodbye—but who gives a fuck?

Drugs are my best friend now; but my lungs really shouldn't be around all of this smoke.

I trade pieces of my body—for pieces of my mind.

☆

Dear Nobody,

The more unhappy I am, the more I want to drink, and right now I REALLY WANT TO DRINK! I'd love some dust or acid right now, or even some 'shrooms. I've been gaining a lot of weight from drinking so much beer—and getting the munchies from all the weed. I must have gained six or seven pounds, but that's okay, it makes me look healthier.

The kids I got high with at the rope swing today were pretty friendly. When Jonathan got ready to leave, he said, "I'll probably see you around this weekend." That's the closest thing I've got to an invitation in months. Being social is hard when you're shy; but now I'm at the point where I JUST DON'T CARE. Oh, I still speak with immense caution, but at least I speak now. What has happened to me? I used to be so free, so open and so expressive. <u>Why doesn't the world act like it knows me?</u>

★

PHOENIXVILLE, PA
EARLY SUMMER, 1997

Dear Nobody,

I didn't see you-know-who today (Jonathan) even though it was pretty nice out. I think I got a little more tan. Tomorrow the weather is supposed to be nice. Maybe more people will be at the rope swing. Maybe I could even get fucked up for free, since mom's stash is still at her friend Jane's house.

I really don't understand any of this. I'm so pretty and even kind of smart (a genius around here, compared to these people) and still I have no boyfriend. Or even an intelligent, mature, pretty female friend. Oh, the stupid boys around here follow me around like little puppy dogs, but none of them with a car, or are intelligent or attractive. It's hard to meet guys like that though. I've been trying since I got here. I'll keep trying until I meet some. And not just a player, either—a nice guy inside.

I'm not stupid, I'm not ugly. I've got to get to the point where I've got no shyness, just reverence. Shyness is ridiculous. Most defense mechanisms are. I guess I've just got to be patient. Things will work out for me. Someone ALWAYS comes along—I've just got to give it time.

Damn, I really wish mom had that pot now. It just takes the edge off, without making me too wild, or too weirded-out.

☿

Dear Nobody,

Trying to make good friends in a new place is one of the hardest things to do, especially for me. I mean, first off, consider how I don't HAVE any friends to make me feel good. Then there's the issue of always having to remember to never be anything less than pleasant, and to be really nice to everyone.

Then there's the matter of not coming on too strong; not to mention having to remember to always pay attention and be polite when the other person speaks—and never put down their opinion. Even if they are a little mean, or rude, pretend not to notice—be even <u>nicer</u> to the ones like that.

Always look good. Dress right. Laugh right.

Always mention the deepness of my voice so that they know I know what or who I sound like already (thank you very much). Remember not to put myself down, so they don't think I've got low self-respect, because then they would get low respect for me (even if I WAS just joking).

When getting high, always remember mom—<u>AND HOW ANNOYING SHE CAN BE WHEN SHE IS HIGH</u>—and engrave it into my brain NOT to act like that.

Make eye contact with everyone in the group, not just a few people. Don't stare. Don't talk too much.

Hide scars.

Don't try to prove I know more about something than someone else (even if I do).

Don't swear too much. Don't spit. Stand up straight.

Talk to people (so I'm not mistaken for a snob) but don't

talk too loud. Don't complain. Don't ask too many questions, but don't NOT ask questions, or they'll think you're not interested. Don't brag. Don't talk about myself too much.

Maybe I should use a defense mechanism? Maybe I should model myself after someone popular, and then when I get friends, slowly unveil my real personality?

No, I am incapable of doing that. I have too forceful a personality. I've just got to remember to exude only my good traits. I'm just too harsh, too dominant, contradictory, and too expressive. I just mean that EVEN AFTER I settle down, I'm still a little EXTRA EXPRESSIVE.

☆

Dear Nobody,

Well, today was pretty fun (for the most part). I met up with some people I know from Reading. We got high and then we all went swimming. THEY all like me. After they left, I saw the people I always usually see down at the rope swing. They were drinking, and let me swig their Zima and vodka. I got pretty toasted. They were being nice, but there was one girl with them who seemed so unapproving of me—or maybe I'm just paranoid?

Oh, then these other cool guys were talking to me. I see them there a lot. Man, sometimes guys can be assholes when they get high. Just like flirting in stupid ways, which I try to ignore. Well, anyway, it was an okay time, even though I did come home feeling a little lonely. Mom went to her sister's and I fell asleep. When I woke up, I listened to records—had my own private party—and then tried on some clothes, and now here I am. Guess I'll go see what's on HBO.

☆

Dear Nobody,

Down at the rope swing last night, I was chilling with these people, they were smoking my pot, and I was drinking their beer (which they got kind of greedy with). We were all getting along okay, but there was that one girl from before, who opposed me being there—seeing as how she kept trying to <u>embarrass</u> me or make me look <u>stupid</u> (which is amplified when I'm fucked-up—so I'm perfectly capable of doing <u>that</u> on my own). Anyway, she kept getting smart with me, and I told her, straight up, that I didn't even know her. She proceeded to humiliate me even more, and then she even dragged some of the boys into it. I was only trying to make them laugh, and defuse some of my ego. But that's probably the problem, EGO—but if I had no ego, I'd never leave the house. Ego is all I pretend I've got, but I always tie it with humor. I don't know, maybe that's the problem? At this point all I've got is myself; and I think I may even be losing me.

Why doesn't my fairy godmother come and rescue me?

Anyway, this bitch got a little jealous of me, and kept on it. Eventually she turned the whole group against me. She knew right where to hit me: "You came here ALONE? Don't you have ANY friends by now?" By the time I left, they were all fucking with me—just saying stupid shit, about my voice and other things. Two guys who I barely know walked me home. I ended up missing what I wanted to watch on TV, but hey, my life's a drama in itself.

I don't know why this girl bothered me so much. What a BITCH. Maybe it's just the area? Maybe the people around here are just RAISED to be extra cruel?

☆

Dear Nobody,

Today was a cloudy, lonely day. I like it much better when the sun is out, and I get to swim. Maybe if I get a tan, I'll look better—and maybe even get a boyfriend. But making new FEMALE friends is the hardest—guys don't have territorial or jealousy issues with nameless, beautiful girls. If I got a "popular" boyfriend (with a car) he could take me to parties—and introduce me to other girls. I never appreciated how hard it is for quiet thinkers to be the new kid. I mean, I always welcomed new kids (that I approved of) to our group with respect and enthusiasm, more than anyone else did. I only wish the favor could be returned (karmically). Well, for now my lonely ass is going to watch 7TH HEAVEN.

★

Dear Nobody,

This guy, Mickey, wants me to come to his house to hear his band. He's only fifteen, and he's a cute little Aquarian, but not really boyfriend-material. Speaking of which, I heard from this girl, Adrienne (AFTER Mickey refused to have sex with her), that Mickey is hung-up on me. It may not even be true, but I'm so desperate and lonely—that I can't help but hope that at least someone might be admiring and thinking of me.

Even if he is kind of a loser.

☆

Dear Nobody,

I just woke up a little while ago. I'm calling my new friend, Adrienne, to go swimming again today. She's okay, I guess, but I'm really hoping Jonathan will be there. People keep saying that Mickey really likes me, but I don't think he's all that hot (they do, I don't). And besides, he's a player—AND he doesn't have a car.

☆

Dear Nobody,

Last night my mom said Mickey called, but I still don't want to go out with him—what if someone better comes along and they hear that I've got a boyfriend? I'm just really hoping for someone older—with a car. I don't know; he's fun to talk to, though. But I guess mostly I don't want to lose Mickey's friendship, especially since I'm kind of short on those. I told him to meet me at the rope swing tomorrow. He said okay. I hope he brings some people with him. I like being there when there's lots of people; the more the merrier.

I LOVE the water. I love to be around all of those negative ions. I can derive power from its strength—it's like a huge hug. When I am swallowed by its still grace, I feel like a human in the most original, natural way. I don't feel like I am on this earth—I feel like I am actually a <u>part</u> of this earth. I swim and move, absorbing power from its ever-changing depths, and I think about all of the creatures, amoebas, insects and bacteria that inhabit this underwater world.

Today the water was clearer than the sky. The further I swam out, the less I could see below me. I could see nothing beyond the surface.

In its deepest, most condensed form, nothing can be seen.

☆

Dear Nobody,

Today, that guy, Zack (that I sorta had a crush on) got landed
on by a girl when she jumped off the rope swing. He'll have
some bruised ribs. Said it hurt a lot. I felt bad for him, but I
don't think I have a crush on him anymore. He's a nice guy,
but his personality doesn't sparkle anymore.

Oh, and I saw that guy, Jonathan, that I smoked dust with
(long hair, white truck). He's okay, but he doesn't talk to me
much. I still wouldn't mind him for a boyfriend, though—but
he doesn't seem interested in me—especially in <u>that</u> way. I
mean, I think I saw him looking at me today, but I feel stupid
when I'm near him. Like he doesn't approve of me or something. Maybe he's how I used to be—quiet but friendly, and
people confuse him for being a snob? Oh, one other thing
is that I always get him fucked-up, and he hasn't gotten me
fucked-up once.

I'm not fucking anyone up anymore. Everyone here
OWES me.

☆

Dear Nobody,

Oh, did I happen to mention that Jonathon likes Andrew Lloyd Webber, and that he love JESUS CHRIST SUPERSTAR?

We listened to it in his truck today.

You know, I'm beginning to believe that there's a good chance Jonathan could be a homosexual...

☆

Dear Nobody,

Even though my mom promised this wouldn't happen—Joe is back living with us. I can't stand the mockery of a woman who I am told is my "mother." Today she told me that she wanted to be with Joe and that if I didn't like it—I should find another place to live. ANOTHER PLACE TO LIVE? I hate her for this. Hate is not a strong enough a word. Over her daughter, she chose a man—a man who beats her in front of her own children, who calls her a whore and a slut. I'm not sure which one of them is sicker? Is it her for taking him back again and again? Or Joe for the way he continues to abuse us?

How am I supposed to deal with this?

I am only human; I am not a force of nature, I am not an angel.

She says she's going to marry him. I scorn her. She doesn't care about me at all. I knew that the time mom and I spent together was too good to be true; it didn't match my life. A mother that loves me? Has time for me? Cares about me? ME? A MOTHER? LOVE?

I am amazed at how much energy she has for him. How much love she gives him. After all she gives him, there's none left for me. They gang up on me. They shame me for every one of their fights. They blame me for everything.

Tomorrow, mom and I are supposed to go to the movies together, but I bet we won't. Joe probably won't allow it.

Dear Nobody,

Today was a good day. Started out shakily, but couldn't have ended better. Okay, first the cops came to our house because mom, Joe and I all got into a fight. It was like an episode of the Jerry Springer Show. Well, after the cops left, I went swimming. A lot of people were at the rope swing. Jonathan was there, but I don't have a crush on him anymore—and this new guy I kinda like, Ryan, wasn't there.

Well, it was a beautiful, sunny day. I have my period, and started to get a headache and tummy ache—and I turned to go home, but then changed my mind. I wanted to go home because I was pissed that Ryan wasn't there, but then I felt better and turned back. And then after a little while, Ryan showed up! I was so happy—it was weird, like it made my whole day! So, I realized today that I've got a HUGE crush on him. Everyone said they saw Ryan looking at me, when I didn't know it. He drives—and he is intelligent—all I need right there!

So I went ahead and told Adrienne and Mickey that I really like him. It is yet to be determined whether or not that was a good move. Probably. Besides, I DO like him! Well, anyway, Ryan can never stay long, so he left pretty early. After he left, we all walked to the Uni-mart and met up with a van full of Adrienne and Mickey's friends. We went to Perkiomenville to this really cool place. It was a bridge with railroad tracks, and if you jumped off the bridge like forty feet, you land in the river. It was awesome.

I got to the ledge but never jumped. I was scared I wouldn't jump out far enough—and hit myself on the rocks. So Adrienne and I waded in. It was SO warm. Unbelievably warm, like a bathtub—literally. I'll never forget how warm it was. The water was even warmer than the air. Then we all went skinny-dipping. It was so fun. Another one of those really excellent days—I've had three so far. I wish summer would never end.

☆

Dear Nobody,

I am starting to be pretty good friends with this one girl, Traci. We've gotten drunk together and she knows all the shit about me, but doesn't care. Me and her have fun. I can be silly with her and just be really weird and she is right back. It's cool. I have a feeling Traci is as loyal a friend as I am. I just wish she lived closer so we could hang out more.

☆

Dear Nobody,

Last night I tried this new drug called, "Special K." It's an animal tranquilizer.

The color of the pills really appealed to me—a bright, electric pink. They reminded me of the birthday parties from when I was little. I always insisted on having bright electric pink balloons. I took all of the eight pills that this guy gave me and washed them down with a 40 ounce of malt liquor. The feeling was NOT what I expected. I didn't feel drugged at all—even though I did feel different. I felt half asleep, half awake.

Whenever I stood up, my knees would go weak and my stomach got that feeling it gets when an elevator suddenly drops.

After a while I started to feel "the stupors." It was harder to remember what my reverie had even been about. I finally started to feel awake and I tried to go to sleep. But I think it was only my mind that felt awake and content—floating like a fallen leaf into one thought, then onto another one—listlessly. My body felt paralyzed—like it does when you wake too suddenly from a dream and you can't move your arm for a few seconds.

After every revelation the room started spinning around with increased velocity. I just lay in bed watching everything spin, unable to concentrate on any single thought. Then I began to see things.

I was staring into the blank television screen and saw a girl speaking sign language so fast it would have been near impossible for anyone to understand. I turned my head away from the hallucination and saw what looked like the silhouette of a tall, lean man opening and closing a door—I looked as closely as I could from where I lay, and tried to tell him to leave.

"Leave me alone," I said. "Please leave me alone."

I was getting scared, seeing a man in my house that I didn't know. At one point I even tried to scream—but I felt so weak that I was having trouble breathing. Every time I caught my breath, I would release it with a sigh. The image of the man finally disappeared, but I kept seeing other things from the corner of my eye. Cats and mice would run across the room. If I stared at an object long enough—the object would begin to smoke. The carpet—WHOOSH, up in flames. My pillow. My dresser. There was fire everywhere. At one point, I thought I saw a snake sliding underneath the carpet. Then everything started to blur together into one big landslide of fuzz.

I kept getting up and leaving the room and then forgetting why I got up in the first place. Then really creepy shit started happening. From the far-off distance I could hear the faint sound of unfamiliar voices—then the room began to spin again and I rolled my head over to the opposite side of the bed facing the curtains. In the curtains I saw a face form under the cloth; then I saw an outline of a body emerge in the fabric. It seemed

to be fighting to get through the curtain. In less than a minute that image faded away and the room went back to spinning.

I spent the next two hours trying to will myself to sleep. I tried counting sheep; I tried counting back from one hundred, spelling out the numbers in my head like they were mathematical figures on a chalkboard. Nothing worked. My thoughts kept fighting with each other. It was like good and evil having a battle.

"Stay up!"

"Go to sleep!"

"Don't listen to HER, don't be a baby, you have to stay up—think of all the incredible ideas and thoughts you are having, do you really want to miss them?

"If you don't go to sleep you will die."

I just laid there letting my two parts fight it out with each other. The sun was coming up when I finally passed out.

$$\maltese$$

Dear Nobody,

I've been hanging out with Traci a lot—she's so great. We do heroin together and get into a lot of trouble—but it's FUN trouble. Kinda. Yeah, I've been doing more drugs lately—but only in moderation.

☆

Dear Nobody,

So I was really drunk and high the other day walking around
with Traci. She wasn't as drunk as I was (no one ever is) and I
was <u>very drunk</u>. And high. VERY HIGH.

We saw these guys at a gas station and asked if they'd give
us a ride further downtown (so we could buy some pot). We
rode around for a while. One was very hot. Turns out they
went to Traci's school. Anyway, they dropped us off by my
house because I wanted (needed) that big bottle of brandy I had
hiding in my closet.

I ran into the house and much to my surprise and dismay,
my mom was already home from work. As soon as she saw me,
she knew I was drunk. She tried to block me (I can't remember
this; it's what she told me later) but I pushed past her and ran
out of the house. After I left, mom called my probation officer
and told him that I was drunk again and had just left the house
without permission.

Meanwhile, Traci and I were walking (crawling) along
Market Street in broad daylight. There was a two-lane highway on the side and we tried to cross it—Traci got across it
fine, but I kept falling over. Cars were beeping their horns
and swerving all around me. A cop in a parking lot across the
street called out to me and asked me if I was okay and if I
could stand up.

I looked around trying to locate the cop car, but I couldn't
really focus. Everything was spinning. "Oh shit," was all I could
think. I'd been puking—and it was all over my face. Then I

fell again, in the middle of the street. A car stopped and people began gathering all around me. I remember how brightly the sun was shining in my eyes. The cop dumped the forty-ounce of beer I had in my hand and took my book bag from me, before arresting me. They let Traci go (I guess because she could still walk, and looked, well, just about normal).

They took me to the ER from there.

My mother was there waiting for me. I was crying, ranting and raving. I kept asking my mom for a quarter to use the payphone, but she kept saying no. I finally got a few dimes from a college kid with a hurt ankle. I called Adrienne and told her to tell Ryan—that no matter what happened, I loved him.

Then some guy came over and told me to go with him. I got a psychological evaluation when I was the most fucked up—and lied my ass off about everything.

They asked me how many times I have had sex and I said, "Twenty-thousand times."

They asked if I ever play with my feces.

I said, "Of course. I eat what I can, and save the rest for later—in the refrigerator!"

Then the shrink left me in a room with a two-way mirror in it for surveillance. Someone had left a dinner tray dinner on a desk, and since I hadn't eaten since 9:00 that morning—and at that point it was around 11:00 at night—I ate the fat off the chicken bones and the cold baked potato (AFTER I got the flies away from it). The doctor must have seen me eating because he came in and asked me if I wanted some crackers or something.

I was very out of it after that, but vaguely recall some old guy driving me to the detention center. The song on the radio was the same song I used to hear almost every time after getting out of the hospital.

When I got there I didn't know where I was and I didn't really care. I was getting so tired. When I first walked into the dayroom I walked into a table and fell. Then I had to strip completely naked (jewelry, too) in front of this nice little woman. Then after my shower I had to answer all of these questions about my history & what brought me there. I was falling asleep while the lady asked the questions. A few hours later they finally let me go to bed.

When I woke up the next morning I didn't know where the hell I was. I could barely remember anything from the night before and wondered why I wasn't wearing my own clothes. I looked like complete shit. I thought maybe I was in some mental ward again. Actually I was kind of glad to be someplace away from home—separate from the ordinary world for a while. I had to clean and mop everything, do anything they told me to. After ten days I was court-ordered to rehab. This place is called the CURON Foundation.

I heard Courtney Love went here.

Excellence in Addiction Treatment™

WERNERSVILLE, PA
SUMMER, 1997

Excellence in Addiction Treatment™

INVENTORY WORKSHEET

Alcohol has brought me here. I never knew alcohol could be such a drug. I guess alcohol isn't really that bad of a drug if you can use it in moderation, but I always wanted more. A lot more.

It took me to heaven, but left me in hell. Every time I drank I walked straight into my own mess—like I was watching it all happen in the third person—like my body and mind were there but my soul was someplace else. When alcohol would mess up a relationship—or something else in my life—I just saw it as more of a reason to drink.

With alcohol, I felt like I was really alive—like I was as good as dead if I was sober. Alcohol became the only thing I had left in my life to live for. The taste and the smell were like magic, working together to comfort me and let me know that soon I would wake up and be alive again—that soon I would be drunk.

I would drink and drink. Throwing up didn't bother me—I felt like it was almost symbolic in how alcohol not only forced all of the bile out of my body, but also forced all of the bile out of my mind. I would be happy and talkative. Loved and laughing. I felt a false spirituality when I drank. I felt like I was on a cloud and I considered everyone my friend.

When an asshole boyfriend did not return my affection, alcohol was there to replace it. When my friends had left me

and taken my esteem along with them, alcohol was there to give me the confidence (or stupidity) to do anything. When my mother was not there to listen, alcohol would always let me talk and not disagree or argue back. When my feelings would hurt me, alcohol destroyed them.

Just the beauty of alcohol proves it is female.

Oh, I miss holding a forty bottle, like it was my infant—but I hadn't conceived it—it had conceived me. And what it made me was either an innocent little girl—giggly and fun—or a raving monster from hell.

Every time I drank, I would feel the little beads of precipitation on the bottle and think of it as the only friend that would ever cry for me. I'd peel off the label like I was unwrapping a present.

I felt secure with alcohol, like I had finally found my home. Alcohol had become my mother, my father, my boyfriend, my best friend and my religion. I drank with a passion. I was always done first and always drunk first—but still wanting more—and if I didn't get it I felt like I was going to die.

It didn't matter how drunk I already was, or how much I had thrown up, or how I couldn't remember what had happened three minutes ago, or where I even was.

With alcohol, I was my own role model. I was never alone,

Excellence in Addiction Treatment™

and she never hurt me. I was obsessed and in love with her. I would lie, steal, beg, and cry for her. I did time for her; I was dying for her.

I hated life, unless I was drunk.

I didn't even want to go to heaven—because I thought I'd have to leave alcohol behind on earth.

Excellence in Addiction Treatment™

Dear Nobody,

I'm trying to be more spiritual. I haven't done drugs or alcohol for thirty days now. I wonder if I will start again when I get out of here tomorrow. Right now, I don't feel like I need it. I'm not desperate, but it only takes a second. Alcohol and drugs can turn me into a disaster, no matter how much of a puritan I want to be. I don't know why. In the long run it just makes me sadder, but I feel so good while I'm in that high. I just wish it didn't suck all the life out of me—and make me feel so empty.

I just want to be happy and drugs don't let me. They make me worry. They make me scared about my future. And paranoid.

But I can fight it!

I can fight anything—if God helps me.

PHOENIXVILLE, PA
SUMMER, 1997

Dear Nobody,

Curon turned out to be complete heaven compared to Detention, but after a while I got sick of it there, too. But I did meet a lot of interesting people. I miss them now. I still talk to two of them—Dylan, and this girl Hayley who is just really down to earth and empathetic (as down to earth as I am, anyway). I just kind of feel like I could trust her. She seems to be really aware—more so than I am (which really isn't saying all that much).

Anyway, now I'm home after like 31 days. Things are more under control and a little better. Nicole is really helping me more than she'll probably ever know. I love her so much. I wish that if I could change one thing, it'd be that Nicole's big sister would have been the one that she deserved.

I remember being eight or nine years old when my half-sister was born. I felt more and more apprehensive the further my mother got into her pregnancy. At first, when she told us she was pregnant (at the dinner table), I felt like it was no big deal. I didn't understand why some of the neighbors and other people were making such a fuss. I didn't really want to be as involved as everyone hoped I would—at least in the beginning. I think I just wanted to enjoy being the only child for as long as I could. But eventually we went to classes at a hospital, and that got me more involved. And sometimes I'd pretend my dolls were my new baby brother. I usually played the baby out as a brother, but I always wanted a sister. Maybe pretending it was a brother made it easier for me to resent the baby—after all, it would be stealing all of MY attention.

Mom's friend Jane took me shopping and bought me a pair of neon-orange sunglasses splattered with black paint. They were gaudy, and had a cord on them so I could wear them around my neck. (I already had a new pair of wine-purple shiny sunglasses with pandas on the corners that my mom bought me, but I didn't tell Jane that.) After shopping, we went to the hospital and I held Nicole and swung back and forth with her. I wanted to hold her for forever. She was my sister (even though I pretended she was MY baby).

My father said that my birth was the loneliest day of his life. My baby sister's birth date was a lonely day for me, but I'd be a lot lonelier without her on every other day of my life. Now, I'm trying to make it up to her.

I'm making up for a lot of things—especially to myself.

☆

Dear Nobody,

I could really like this guy I met at Curon. Dylan's really nice, and cute (for a little guy), but he's not exactly my type. He's younger than me by a year, and I usually go for guys that are two or three years OLDER than I am. But he really is kind of smart, in an intellectual way. He's not exactly um, drug-smart. He does drink, sometimes, but he really shouldn't; I guess he's just not as experienced as I am when it comes to those sorts of things. Maybe I kind of like that?

Dylan's really nice to me, and I know he cares about me. The whole time I was in Curon, he was there with me, keeping me company. I really did like that. He always seems interested in what I have to say. He laughs at my jokes. I like the way he looks at me, and I like the way he looks. And it's not like he's not taller than I am (it's just not by much).

Sometimes I don't always remember promises I've made to him, or to call him when I say I will. But I really like his obstinacy. It shows great camaraderie. That's just what I need right now, too. What I've always needed.

☆

Dear Nobody,

This is my third night home from rehab. When I got home my mother agreed that she would not drink anymore and she would not see Joe—who we both know is her biggest trigger. In rehab, they told me to stay away from people and places. Since I've been home, I haven't spoken to any of those triggers—I can control myself—but can my mom?

Tonight Joe called while I was on the other line with Dylan. I said, "I'm on the other line," and he told me to tell mom that he had called.

That's like asking me to tell my mom to put me through HELL all over again.

It's like telling her to go ahead, and get drunk in front of me—go ahead and embarrass me and yourself in front of everyone.

It's like telling her to go ahead and wreck the car because you're too drunk to drive again. It's like telling her to go ahead and not come home until the next morning again.

It's like telling her to go ahead and scrape up your knees again, or bruise your legs again from falling because you were too drunk to walk, again.

It's like telling her to go ahead and dress yourself up as a whore and bring some stranger back home with you so you can screw around on the couch, while I walk in on you and you're too drunk to care.

It's like telling her to go right ahead and fill the refrigerator with beer when there's no food in the house.

It's like telling her go ahead and hang out at some shitty bar while her daughter sits at home all alone, crying because she feels so lonely.

It's like telling her to go ahead and choose alcohol over her daughter.

So I didn't give her Joe's message.

☆

Dear Nobody,

So my mother comes into my room tonight and asks, "Why do you have glue in your room?" Excuse me, I was in rehab for drinking, NOT HUFFING. Okay, I got a little disgruntled, but I let it roll off of my back. I went downstairs to talk to my grandma, and she asked who I had been on the phone with, and I told her, "Dylan." She said in a real smart-ass, bitchy-tone, "Yeah, right," like he was my imaginary friend or something. It was just too much; I ran up to my room to cry.

I wanted to handle this normally, but my mom was at the bottom of the steps telling me to come down and do my homework. I told her I was upset and asked if she could please come upstairs and talk to me alone—because I could not address my feelings with my grandma there. But my mother had to play one of those power struggle bullshit games. She said that we could talk on the stairs, IF I came to the bottom of the steps— two feet away from her room.

The point was that she would talk to me on the steps, which was less than halfway to my room, and would have ALMOST been in my room, but would not actually come into my room, so we could talk. Power Struggle!

Mom knew we would be discussing unpleasant subjects so she played one of those games. I guess nothing's changed for her.

P.S.—She's on the phone with Joe right now.

WOW, IT'S SO GOOD TO BE HOME!

⭐

Dear Nobody,

I've been talking to Dylan all night. We feel the same about so many things. We've also got something in common; he has juvenile arthritis in his knees—and I have it in my hips and knees. I've been in traction, a wheelchair, and crutches. I don't know how severe it was for him, but I do know that he was put on Codeine for it. I'm glad he's got some idea what's going on with me—and I haven't even told him <u>anything</u> yet. Maybe he'll understand more than the assholes around here. I'm devoting my life to music and books. I hate people. I can't love them—they hurt me way too bad—even more than my poor knees do.

☆

PHOENIXVILLE, PA
LATE SUMMER, 1997

Dear Nobody,

Dylan lives in Gettysburg, so I only see him on the weekends, but we talk every day. We slipped up today—and got drunk together. Just a few beers. But when I got home, my mother could tell. That's okay, though—I think she still drinks, too. Except now she keeps it in moderation. I doubt I'll seriously drink anymore either. Time will tell—but I <u>definitely</u> won't binge anymore.

☥

Dear Nobody,

HA! That resolution lasted three days! Now I get drunk as a skunk, every day. I don't even go to school. I love Dylan now, even though I promised myself we would just be friends—and we are doing as many drugs as I can get. Mom's back together with a man that abuses her and tried to kill her. They both have alcohol problems—and yesterday I got high with my mom for the second time!

☆

Dear Nobody,

I can't believe I came home drunk last night! I just got out of rehab a few weeks ago. God help my family, they are SO disappointed. I haven't talked to them yet, but I know what to expect. And to top it all off—my grandparents are still here. It's the next morning and I'm up in my room—too ashamed to come downstairs, even though I have the traditional thirstiness, and need to piss really badly. When my mom gets up, I'll talk to her.

But I'm kind of glad, because at least when I drank—it was recreational this time.

☆

Dear Nobody,

Well, it's final. I have a huge crush on that guy, Ryan. I'm not sure if he likes me. I want to take things VERY slowly. Only because I like him so much. The thing is, he's not even all that attractive. He's kind of thin, even—but I like him. A LOT. I think he might be really smart. Mature. He's seventeen, I think. He seems so gentle. It's touching just to watch him watching nature. He's never blatantly disrespectful to anyone. I've never heard him degrade a female. He's interested in art, and likes the same music that I do. I've never really seen him stare at me, but I do think I saw him look at me once or twice. But then again, he does that to everyone—in his deep, analytical way.

Dear Nobody,

Ryan was not at the rope swing today. He ought to be ashamed of himself—leading an innocent, trusting girl (like me) on like that! But today was a pretty nice day anyway. Made me feel pretty again. Like, <u>really</u> pretty. Even though Ryan never came, OTHER guys were there, and they renewed my sense of self-beauty. I just KNEW they liked me, even though no-one really got my number—though they DID ask. Ryan will come back for me though. Hopefully tomorrow.

☆

Dear Nobody,

I don't just like Ryan, I adore him. <u>Admire</u> him. I am almost <u>obsessing</u> over him. I want to see his life. I want to be IN his life. I just hope this isn't the sort of thing where I like Ryan more than he likes me. That'd be kind of upsetting.

Man, aren't I pathetic? No, not as much as some teenage girls are—but that's not saying much! At least I'm not boy-crazy.

I really like him. Dammit!!! This sucks, SUCKS, **sucks**.

I just REALLY, REALLY, REALLY hope he's there tomorrow.

♡

Dear Nobody,

Well, I just got back from the rope swing, and guess what? Ryan (my would-be soul mate) showed-up. And not only does he show-up—but he shows up with <u>another girl!</u> Not just any girl either—a really pretty hippie-girl. She had long blonde hair and a really pretty face; really beautiful blonde hair, and even more beautiful blue-green eyes. All of the girls that come down to the rope swing have hair like that—blonde—with eyes as clear and light as the sky in August. She looked older, and cooler than I do (I guess)—more like his type (I have dark brown hair, to match my even darker brown eyes).

I think I acted a little cold to him—after I saw him with that other girl. After that Ryan kind of ignored me. I wondered WHY he had brought her? That pissed me off a lot. I was upset—even a little devastated. I still hope he's there tomorrow, even though he kind of ignored me today. ALONE though. Maybe I could find out who she is and what she means to him? This sucks—I thought about Ryan A LOT; and I still think about him. He's everything I've kept my eye open for (not looking really—I'm never REALLY looking). Though I like him, A LOT. **A LOT!**

☆

Dear Nobody,

Tonight I dyed my hair blonde, but I knew it wouldn't turn out "blonde" after being dark brown—it turned out kind of sandy-butterscotch. The peroxide totally burnt my scalp. I just hope Ryan appreciates it. Even if he doesn't appreciate it, I hope that he at least LIKES it. I do. It's a great color. I mean, it didn't exactly turn out BLONDE, but I didn't expect it to—my hair is way too dark. I had to look at it for a while to get used to it, but now I like it okay. As matter of fact, I love it!

Of course, when Ryan sees it, I'll have to scorn it profusely, saying I hate it, and that it came out all wrong. You know, just in case he doesn't like it—he'll just think that I messed up, and that I must look even better, when it turns out right.

Oh, man, this is how it started last time, remember? First it's the little things; like how you accept the way he'll make you feel stupid when you talk too much. Then it's how he always forgets money when we go out, and I pay. Or when he has money, he'll buy himself food, or pay his own way, and not offer to pay mine.

It all starts with how he'll look me over, and I'll feel criticized, not admired. And that's when I start changing myself, dying my hair, buying new clothes, and just hoping that he'll like it.

Then comes even more serious self-sacrifice, for the sake of HIS happiness, until it doesn't even BRING him happiness, until it's just expected—until nothing matters—but HIM being sure that I am always there.

But I still really hope he likes my hair. I bet the sun will make it a little bit lighter. It IS unusual.

I just feel so out of place. Even the dark-haired people around here have clear green or blue eyes. Maybe I'll get contacts, blue ones. I mean, I've already dyed my hair. I don't know, maybe I shouldn't even have done that. Oh, what do I care? Well, around here, I guess <u>I have to.</u>

I REALLY want friends. I hate this.

Today I cleaned my room because mom said she'd take me to the mall if I did. Maybe I could get her to buy me some hippie clothes (the people around here dress like hippies). Maybe then I'd be "cool."

See how desperate I am?

I keep thinking about Hayley, the girl I met at Curon. I'd write her a letter if I weren't so fucking lazy...

☆

Dear Nobody,

Well, today was my first day at the rope swing as a blonde. It was, um, interesting. First of all, I felt a little more confident in myself. I was less shy. I had fun. Ryan was there, but he had no comment on my hair.

I'm crushing on him. Yeah, I'm crushing on him.

There's a heat-wave going on now (supposed to be even hotter tomorrow) and I met some pretty nice people (and guys). Some of the guys down there are SO obvious when they flirt.

Man, I really had hopes for Ryan—he's STILL my crush. I could fall in love with this guy. I can't remember feeling this much adoration for any guy. See, he and I are both reserved, a little quiet, and probably try to avoid emotionally embarrassing and/or risky situations (well, I may not be tranquil, but I'm certainly tenacious).

I have no idea if he crushes on me too.

Probably, not as much as I crush on him.

That's why it's called a crush.

More often than not, I get crushed.

Dear Nobody,

I'm supposed to meet Mickey at the rope swing around 1:00 p.m. tomorrow. When Mickey is there, we usually see Ryan, but after the faces I made the other day, and the mood I was in, Ryan may never be interested in me again—if he ever was. Story of my life. I should have just played it off sweetly, gushing blind friendliness towards Ryan—and making friendly chatter with his "girlfriend," by complimenting her on her many beautiful physical attributes. That would have fed my vengefulness, and really fucked with him; but I'm just not like that anymore. Instead, I openly sulked, brooded and feigned disinterest in him. I occasionally glanced in HER direction—to size her up. I think he may have seen that. Oh fucking well. I'm not even all that hurt any more. Maybe it's just PMS.

I know he'll be back. Sooner or later.

My magnetism can't be that easy to resist.

Adrienne's boyfriend did help console me, though. Even though I was above asking—he said I looked <u>better</u> than the girl my crush had brought—that I was beautiful.

☆

PHOENIXVILLE, PA
LATE SUMMER, 1997

Dear Nobody,

Hooray! Ryan asked me out today! I went to the rope swing figuring I wouldn't see him at all. I didn't even wash my hair, and I wore the same red dress over my bathing suit that I had worn the day before. I offered him a beer and we got to talking. His girlfriend wasn't there. Maybe they broke up? I hope so, but even if they were still together, I still would have said "yes" (just to test him out).

Mickey gave me the silent treatment for the rest of the day, but I didn't care.

I was on cloud nine.

Dear Nobody,

I've got to reconstruct myself. I've got to evolve, and regenerate. That must be why I was sent here to Phoenixville; my destiny wants me to reclaim my true self. I COULD be freer here—I could, maybe, even be comfortable. The ties I bind here could be strong, maybe even honest. I FEEL it—if I could get past the obstructive nature of adolescent relationships, I could build an even more powerful empire. I've got new energy; a new opposition to my previous thinking.

I'm excited now that I know my fate. I cannot sleep tonight (today—it's 6:00 a.m.—and no sleep so far since yesterday). Now, I need my dreams; they have led me to my conclusion (thank you, God). I need them now to unleash the strategy behind my façade (and I need sleep if I expect to keep up this marvelous energy). I've just got to remember to be nice and warm-hearted in my overall relations to people. If I feign shyness and waste my given energy, I will only become restless, which can be very counterproductive to this new "Life Project."

☆

Dear Nobody,

I've fallen in love with Ryan. Hard. We all were down at the rope swing with mom's boyfriend, Joe, drinking a case of beer—I had like eight beers and Ryan had three. Joe was drinking whisky and told Ryan I liked him. It was okay—at least we got it established. Ryan seemed okay with it, but really didn't show if he liked me—though he did seem a little more comfortable around me after that. Well, since I was getting a buzz on (even though I <u>wasn't</u> drunk) I was getting loud. Okay: loud, bossy and cursing A LOT, but I was still okay. Ryan seemed to want to leave, but I wouldn't let him. I told him he had to stay—so he did. Then he said that he HAD to go home because he needed to get up EARLY the next day, so he could get his picture taken <u>for yearbook.</u>

I asked him if he planned on going to the rope swing tomorrow.

He said, "Yeah."

I asked, "What time?"

He said that it would depend on what time he woke up!

DUH! He can't even lie right.

Oh, well.

So guess what—the next day, he doesn't even show up! At ALL! So I got really, really drunk. **MAD DRUNK**. I went to Adrienne's and called him to bitch him out. Ryan hung up on me when I started yelling. When I called back his mom answered and told me that Ryan wasn't there—even though she's as bad a liar as her son—I was still really polite.

Man, I done fucked up. Haven't heard from Ryan since. Fucker. Oh well.

I STILL like him though.

☆

Dear Hayley,

Hi Hayley! How's it going? So much fucked-up shit has been happening to me—I don't even know if it's all good or all bad. I don't know if I should be happy or freak the fuck out! Well, I've been getting fucked-up, "for free," everyday lately and I've been making acquaintances and I fall in love with a new person every day. But there's this one guy, Ryan, that I just can't seem to shake. He's so placid and tranquil—a thinker—like you, Hayley. One thing I'm not—is placid, and I've NEVER been described as tranquil. Passionate, and uh, ambitious—okay, I guess; whereas you two may be more analytical, where I would be more curious. Understand? Well I'm telling you this because you would get it more than anyone else. So for the past few weeks, we've been talking, and throwing "glances" at each other. It took him a while, but I got some of his ice to break, and his natural warmth melted most of mine. I was still usually quieter around him, but when he came around, everyone else vanished and HE became my audience. And what do I do for an audience?

Perform!

Well, one day my mom's boyfriend got drunk, and came down to where we usually hang out. He bought us a case of beer. We were all drinking—I had eight beers in about forty-five minutes (maybe an hour). I wasn't drunk, just buzzing a little.

My mom's boyfriend was the most fucked-up. He looked at my crush and asked Ryan if he had a job, and when "my" guy said, "No" mom's boyfriend said, "Well, Mary Rose really likes you, so you bet you have a job now!"

Let me say that when I drink, I like to BE the party—I make jokes and inspire the drunken debates of conversation more than anyone else in the room. Well, I was in rare form compared to what my crush was used to seeing of me. He laughed at all of my jokes, and I caught him looking at me, but maybe that was in shock, since I was being so contrary to my "usual" self. Ha—I was getting pretty drunk as the night progressed. I borrowed somebody's shirt, and I threw up all over it. Ryan was watching. I didn't want to gross him out, but I had to sit down. Somebody goes, "SHE'S PUKING ALL OVER YOUR SHIRT!"

I go, "I'm not puking on it, I'm CUSTOMIZING it!"

Everyone laughed and so did he.

Well, a while later I started getting bitchy and bossy, but had a sense of humor about it. I don't think he expected me to be the type to get rowdy. But I was. VERY rowdy. We had fun, but I don't think he expected it.

Long story short, I caught him in a lie, but I acted like I didn't notice. That disappointed me—nothing hurts like being lied to. But I surprised him a few times that night with my deceptiveness—but <u>I didn't lie</u>. So I figure we're even, and I crush on him even more, now that I'm comfortable with him. Well, it turns out the next day (after the night of surprises) Ryan stands me up.

I was <u>devastated</u>.

So I did the only reasonable thing I could think of—I got even drunker than the night before, and called Ryan and cursed him out until he hung up on me (another thing he probably thought me not capable of). He thought I was "above" that I guess. You know; like I was ultra-passive or something. NOT when I'm drunk. So when he hung up, I called right back and his mom answered and said he wasn't there. She probably guessed I was fucked-up. Ryan was probably pissed.

<u>Yep, looks like I blew that one.</u>

So I go get this cute guy that I'm attracted to, but wouldn't "date," and we were making out in my basement. When my mom got home, I guess she was locked out of the house, and I was too busy to hear her knocking on the door, so she breaks a window to get in—and found us. She wasn't that pissed, but we left anyway. I came home late that night, and woke up around four a.m. under the coffee table in the living room. I was still fucked-up.

My mom comes downstairs and says, "What are you doing?"

I said, "Leave me alone, I'm camping."

See, I'm weird when I'm drunk, but at least I have a sense of humor about it.

Anyway, guess I scared the shit out of Ryan. So much for pretending to be tranquil; should have been myself from the start. I wanted Ryan to like me—no matter how much it hurt. So now I end up with the one I could love, shaking his head like, "What the fuck?" and some guy I just thought was cute—is almost in love with me.

I call it karma. It all balances out.

Maybe Ryan just needs time to digest what's been going on. Besides, once I get in somebody's system, it's pretty hard to get me out completely.

Ryan has a Virgo mom, and you're a Virgo, so maybe you'd be able to help me with him.

Okay, well I love you tons, and miss you tons!

Love forever,

Mary Rose

Dear Nobody,

Well, today mom pulled some crazy shit. We were getting along so well. We were hanging out together, being a family; almost like when I was little. So I get back from the rope swing and there's a note on the table saying that she went to meet Joe and that she'd be back at 7:30 p.m. Well after 7:30 (a LOT after), mom comes home with my McDonald's dinner, and surprise—Joe—her abusive ex-boyfriend (or fiancé—or whatever) was with her! I was SO ENRAGED! So when they were out on the porch smoking cigarettes, blowing smoke into **MY** house, I locked them out. Deadbolt, wood stick, locked windows. And I barricaded the front door with furniture. They were out there for two hours before Joe started yelling something and got a garden tool and tried to pry through the kitchen window. That's when I threw her wallet and keys out the window and they left.

Mom called from a payphone. She told me if I didn't like living there with him, I would, "HAVE TO FIND SOMEPLACE ELSE TO LIVE!" Yep. My own "mother" chose an abusive, asshole boyfriend over me and my eight-year-old sister. Fucking bitch! She only loves me when it's convenient. I'M the one who is always there for her. I'M the one who is her DAUGHTER—and that word means nothing to her.

She said she was driving him two hours back to his parents' house; that's four hours of driving for that asshole.

Well, its 3:20 a.m. and she still isn't home yet. I hate it—how

104

dare she choose him over my baby sister and me? HOW? She cannot possibly love me. At all. She causes me so much pain. I could deal with my life if it weren't for her. I'm just a human after all. I've got my plate full. And I already feel like vomiting.

All I ever need is love. Just love. Love makes me happy.

I mean, now that Joe's gone, I feel okay, I guess. So long as he stays gone. But I am still very hurt. Very hurt, but okay for now. Well it's almost 3:30 a.m. (ten more minutes) and she still isn't home. So nice she can take off work for such things, but when we've got plans or something, she has to work—undoubtedly.

Oh well, from now on I'll just focus my energy on fun, nice things. But for now—I'm going to bed to try and sleep.

☦

Dear Nobody,

I just did some dope that some guy from Reading gave me.

I feel like the star of my own movie.

I feel like the queen of my own Queendom.

I feel like the prize of everyone's game.

I feel like the model of my own designs. I feel like the diamond in a musty cave.

Oh, how indescribable; I could be the author of a million theses and still not be able to describe this...

☆

Dear Nobody,

Its 6:00 a.m. Here I am—still buzzing from last night.

I'm buzzing so hard that I can barely feel my fingertips.

I had better be sleeping. I've got school in a couple of hours.

I took my picture twice with my new camera. I look pretty (but fucked up).

I can't remember coming home. I think Traci's parents gave me a ride.

I love alcohol. I love pictures.

I love pictures of me and alcohol.

I wonder if I did any drugs last night?

I look so pretty.

Its 6:05 a.m. Shit its early.

I'd better go to sleep while I can.

Good morning!

★

Dear Nobody,

Well Mary Rose, you are so fucked up right now. Heroin. Sweet heroin. Look, I can't even write I'm so fucking high. I'll...

Dear Nobody,

Okay, that was last night. I'm not high now, but I was then (<u>DUH!</u>).

☆

Dear Nobody,

Man, I'm losing my tan. I used to be REALLY tan until I
started sleeping all day and only going out at night. Maybe I
should start going to bed earlier so I can get up and go out in
the sun? Well, we'll see.

☆

Excellence in Addiction Treatment™

WERNERSVILLE, PA
LATE SUMMER, 1997

CURON FOUNDATION

Excellence in Addiction Treatment™

Dear Hayley,

Have I got a story for you! Let me begin at the beginning, and when I get to the end, I'll stop. Remember when you called me a few months ago to tell me that your friend had died, and how you thought there was some bad dope going around the east coast? Well, you were right—right as rain.

It was a Sunday. I woke-up really hung-over with scrapes all over my knees, elbow, and hands—and I was covered in black mud. I must have fallen down a hill—because the night before I had gotten extremely drunk AND I'd been tripping on micro dots. I wished I was still tripping, and wanted to buy more, but I had no beans. So I went down into the basement and got those six beers left over from the night before. I drank them all before I left the house. Then I went to the woods, where people hang out on the trails and just chill and get fucked up, or swim (it's by a river).

My usual asshole acquaintances were there—none of them who would know a drug besides pot or alcohol if it fucked them up the ass. But then on the other side of the trail was a group of college kids, so I went over and started talking to them. They were getting more alcohol, so they said they would bring me back a forty ounce—and when they came back—they brought this girl with them. The girl, **Vickie**, didn't stay long, but before she left,

113

she asked me if I wanted to go into Philly with her to get dope. I finished my forty, and off we went. By then I was buzzing, but I still really wanted dope.

When we got to the city, her dealer sold her one or two bags. He gave me one to be nice (because I was sick), and she was a good customer. Well, it was the first time I ever booted myself up and I don't know if I felt much effect at the beginning—the part that's supposed to be like, "WHOA"—because alcohol numbs, and I was <u>almost</u> drunk. Regardless, I felt good— better, at least.

We drove back to Phoenixville to meet up with her friend, **Geoff**, and after awhile we all decided to go back into Philly to get some more dope. On the way we stopped at my house and I snagged twenty dollars from my mom's purse (I still feel really bad about that) and we were on our way, again.

Geoff bought two bags. My new girlfriend, Vickie, bought one. I bought two (me being my dumb-ass self). Geoff booted up first—then Vickie went. I wanted to wait. I KNEW I should wait, but I was so impatient, that I asked him to boot me up with both of my bags. Geoff did and I felt really good. The heroin was called OAK TREE. I started to nod off, and when I opened my eyes it was night time. About fifteen minutes had gone by, but it felt more like an hour. I remember the guy slapping my face trying to wake me up, but I just kept nodding off.

The next thing I remember is being in some parking garage getting lifted from the back seat into a wheelchair.

I remember lots of yelling and when I opened my eyes I was being wheeled into an emergency room. Then I remembered the nurses taking my clothes off and all these people around me. It was like that TV show "E.R."

These are the bits and pieces that I remember: I remember my mom coming in and crying. I remember the machines beeping. I remember coming down, or back to, whatever...My mom told me that my grandpop came in all the way from New Jersey, because they thought I was going to die. I don't remember that.

Then the doctors put me in an ambulance and sent me to another hospital. I barely remember the ambulance ride. When I got to the other hospital I went back to sleep, but I woke up when one of the machines started beeping. A nurse ran in. I was going back into respiratory distress. They put these oxygen canals on me and equipment to monitor my heart. I remember trying to tear them off. Then I fell back asleep.

I still felt high the next day; my pupils were still the size of pin-points. But I came down, eventually (unfortunately), and the hospital said they had to send me to a residential treatment center for insurance reasons. Of course I fiercely refused, but I'm not eighteen, and they threatened to have me committed. So I agreed to go.

Excellence in Addiction Treatment™

And guess where I ended up? THE CURON FOUNDATION!
<u>Again</u>.

Can you believe it? It sucks here so BAD. I'll be here
for fourteen days. They call it "stabilization."

If I thought this place was bad before—now it's even
worse—it's like Concentration Camp Curon. The staff has changed
and the rules are much stricter. We don't even have rec with the
guys, and for cigarette breaks—we have to go on the other side
of the building. But that's not all. The people who were in last
time were like way cooler then the asshole losers in here now. The
boys aren't even that attractive (with the exception of one,
but he's full of himself). We never get to look at them anyway.
Only one other girl, besides me, is in here for dope. ONE OTHER
GIRL!!! The rest of them are just like these preppy little
bitches that got drunk or smoked pot once or twice—before their
mommy and daddy found out and sent them to rehab. So as you
can imagine, I feel VERY lonely.

I know you know how it feels to be here—missing dope and not
being able to relate to anyone because they're all so fucking lame.

Fucking Nurse Janis put me on three hour isolation today,
because she heard I was talking during a lecture. Who THE FUCK
do I have to talk to? I'm so lonely here. It's like living with all
those bitchy, preppy girls from high school that ever called me a
freak and tried to make me feel inferior and less of a human being.

CURON FOUNDATION

Excellence in Addiction Treatment™

Sometimes people's cruelty just shocks me so much—that I start to think that it must be me? Sometimes I feel paranoid

because I had a bad trip a while ago, and I don't know if the paranoia just decided to stay, or if I'm just being realistic?

I bet I'm just being realistic.

And those little bitches can bet their cardboard lives that if they keep fucking with me, I'll give them something "realistic."

Fuck man, nobody even stays up at night. Just me. Oh, I'm so pissed off and lonely here. Nobody understands me here. Fucking SHIT! I wish I could just call you. I can't even call my mom. Well, I should go. Fucking lights out. I'm sitting on the bathroom floor with the light on so I can see what I'm writing—this is so fucked up.

Please don't forget about me. I love you forever.

XOXOXO

Mary Rose.

PS. I wish you were here (!)

(Just kidding—kinda.)

Dear Nobody,

I want to go home. I hate this place. Well, maybe not home—
but definitely not here. It has been seven days since I got here.
Seven days since I last did heroin.

I hate the showers here. These towels are so harsh—they
feel like sandpaper. My skin feels raw. Today after I did my
chores and they let me shower, I put my leg up on the metal
towel rack to dry off my skin. When I put my foot on it—the
rack slid down a little and I noticed the loose screws track-
ing scratches that were already on the wall. Somebody must
have put their foot up there before. Someone else in rehab—
someone probably just like me.

As I dried that leg, I noticed the bruises on it. There are
bruises everywhere on my body. I don't know how any of
them got there, except for maybe the few on my arms. I always
told myself that I'd never shoot up—but deep down inside of
myself, I knew I was lying. I've gotten pretty good at that.

So here I am—dripping and naked in a bathroom without a
mirror in a drug rehab. It's not like I need a mirror anyway. I
know I'm ugly—but I haven't always been this ugly.

The dirt under my nails is as black as charcoal—and there is
so much of it that it's like my fingernail is clinging to the dirt,
rather than the dirt clinging to my fingernails. The palms of my
hands are torn open. I think I got most of the rocks out. I'm
watching the bones moving under the skin on the top of my
hand. They look like little strings—and my fingers the puppets
that dance at the ends of them. The scrapes on my elbows and

knees look like little muddy streets disguised as wounds. Maybe I've got a world on my body and the scabs are its streets now.

I wonder if there are any drugs on my streets?

☆

PHOENIXVILLE, PA

FALL, 1997

Dear Nobody,

Alright, I haven't written in this book for a while. Well, since August, when I overdosed on heroin and went back to rehab for two weeks. Anyway, when I got out, that guy, Geoff, and the girl, Vickie, found me again. That was cool. Sure surprised me. The guy, Geoff, is cool, and Vickie, that's his best friend, and now she's my friend, too. So it's like October now, and we've been hanging out ever since. We've gone to lots of raves and shit since then.

Dear Nobody,

Last night I got FUCKED UP, because I thought that I wouldn't be doing dope for a while, because today I was starting some outpatient rehab in Wyomissing, and was going to stick with it for six weeks. Well, I went there today, and it's all fucked up. It's supposed to be with other kids my age, but no other kids my age are enrolled. So I'm supposed to be the only one in an adolescent lecture group—but since I'm an adolescent, I'm the only one in my group?

Uh, no, I don't think so.

I don't mind going to meetings and shit, but this place is just STUPID. No wonder I'm the only one going. It might not have been that bad if other kids went (like the program said).

Back home, I like hanging out with Geoff and Vickie, but all they ever want to do is get high. Not like there's anything wrong with that (like I can talk or something), but school started last month.

DAMMIT!

☆

Dear Nobody,

So, Geoff's kind of like my boyfriend now. When he's drunk he tells me how much he thinks about me. When he's sober he doesn't talk to me at all. But I'm not sure—I think he might really like me.

He's been away for a few days and I wonder if he still feels the same? I heard absence makes the heart grow fonder. I say, "Out of sight—out of mind." I haven't talked to him since last week anyway, so who gives a shit. He hates talking on the phone. AND he refuses to talk to me if I am pissed at him. But I don't mind.

I REALLY like him.

Oh, and he's a virgin!

I can't wait to break him in!

※

Dear Nobody,

Well, its 2:30 p.m. and I'm waiting for this movie to be over so I can get ready to go out tonight. Hmm, I really have to get a job. This going out every night is getting pretty expensive.

☆

Dear Nobody,

Um, okay, so I'm just sitting here, watching a movie. Its quarter to ten. I should be out with you-know-who, but Geoff called earlier to say that he was sick and there's no way he's leaving his house tonight.

Man, it sucks, because I got all dressed up and I look kind of extra nice.

Oh, well, there's always going to be tomorrow…

☆

Dear Nobody,

So, I've fucked Geoff two and a half times so far. It didn't really count the third time—because it was only for, like, two seconds. The other times were a little longer—kinda. One time I passed out (when we were right in the middle of it) and he got mad at me. So last night I got really wasted and hung out with his friend, Sam. Sam is really cool; I think he's like the perfect person. He and I started kissing and it was TOTALLY fun. Sam's really ugly, but we had sex anyway—just so I could piss Geoff off. Later I told Geoff about it, but I don't think he really cared.

Too bad I'll be dead soon—or I'd fuck all his friends and REALLY try to hurt him.

☆

Dear Nobody,

Yeah, I fucked your best friend
I know your pissed, don't pretend
Ha, ha, ha, I fucked your friend
Who's the one laughing in the end?
I'm the queen heartless bitch
Your friends all want me, it doesn't matter which
Yeah, I fucked your best friend
And I liked him more
Because I'm the best-revenge-whore
I fucked your best friend
Now he'll have the stories to tell
Because I fucked you both straight to hell
I fucked your best friend
And now he wants me more
He's not really your friend and I made sure
I fucked your best friend
Because for you it is too late
Now you can think of who I'm fucking when you masturbate.

★

Dear Hayley,

Right now there are 27 rolls of film in my book bag that I need to develop. They're from last weekend, and it's so strange because that weekend I spent in a flop-house with people I thought hated me. Sam and Vickie got kicked out of it because I got in a fight with someone that was being an ass... Okay, I threw a bottle at my ex-boyfriend Geoff, because he was sitting on the couch when I walked in.

Anyway, at this other club, the girl who decided who can come in and who can't come in—almost didn't let me in, because when she met me last summer—I was puking everywhere and so fucked up that I couldn't walk. I didn't remember it, but apparently SHE DID. Anyway, we got in for free, but they only let Sam in because HE had money. I know, doesn't make any sense to me either.

Well, I walked in and I'm telling everyone about the other club we just got back from (the Tabernacle). Sam and Vickie wouldn't dance, so I was dancing with these really nice gay guys instead. A few girls danced with me, but everyone else was looking at me and rolling their eyes or laughing at me. Sam and Vickie were in a corner the whole time while I danced. I have pictures, but they may not turn out, because it was so dark in there. I really hope they do. Anyway, after we left, on our way to that flop-house, I asked Sam, "why were people acting so weird toward me?"

And can you believe this—he told me it was just because I look "punk-ish," and that it was a "GOTH" club!!!

How fucking ridiculous!

Well, I had fun anyhow.

Miss you,
Love Forever,

Mary Rose

Dear Nobody,

I got a job to pay for all this going out—at McDonalds. FUCK that place. I hate it there. I dropped out of school, so now I work a forty-hour work-week. Eight hours a day. My boss is a real asshole. Fuck him, too. He's this bitchy little queer that's always screaming at me until I cry. Fuck HIM. Or "her." Whatever IT wants to be—fuck it either way. Anyhow, I haven't shown up for the past two days. I'll get suspended if I do it one more time.

FUCK IT.

I also got in a fight with Geoff, and we haven't talked for forever. I mean we got in this huge fight. BIG. And he's the only one with the car. Vickie <u>had</u> a car—but it broke down one night. Yeah, that was fun. **NOT!** Anyway, maybe I'll call him and apologize. Now that I have this job and all, I want to go out and spend money. But I don't want to do it alone. I'll call him tomorrow—maybe. I'll definitely call Vickie though; maybe she can hang out with me...

☆

Dear Nobody,

Geoff and I kind of made-up today. I was the one that called him—I wonder if he feels how I do? I'm sure I love him—in some fucked-up way. I just feel like he can't really be honest with me. I'm honest with him (for the most part). It's just so hard not to fuck up. See, I used to get so pissed at him for the little things he did, but now it's like I spend more time apologizing to HIM. And it's like he always already knows when I've done something stupid, like he's got fucking sonar or something.

I know that he and his friends think I'm some crazy, slutty, dirty bitch. But I really don't care that much because they really are assholes. But I'd give anything to see what Geoff says or does if they talk shit about me. He probably fucking goes right along with them. I don't know, maybe I deserve it.

Oh shit, I miss him. I haven't seen him for a while, and on the phone, I'm always the one talking, and he just plays his music and kinda ignores me. Most times, I'm not even sure he's listening to me. Maybe he likes me for something besides the person I am? I'm not sure.

God I love him. It's just like every once in a while, he'll say something really brilliant and pretty, and I'll think of how amazing he is.

Then he'll say something really stupid and I'll think he's fucking retarded.

☆

Dear Nobody,

I got my first paycheck and spent most of it partying with Geoff. The rest I lent to him (or his friends). Last night, he didn't have enough money to get fucked up with because he'd just bought a new car—so I helped him out a little—like I'd been doing ALL WEEK. Then, even after my immense generosity, Geoff asked to borrow MORE money. I told him, no, that I still wanted to hold on to some of my money, but that I would at least give him gas money. THAT wasn't enough for him. He got a really smart-ass tone with me—and began to raise his voice. It was embarrassing because he was yelling at me in his garage and his folks were home.

<u>All I wanted was to have a good night.</u>

So I told him that, but stuck to my decision about not lending him any more money. Well, he flipped the fuck out! I mean BLEW UP! He suddenly screamed at me, "YOU SELFISH, SPOILED LITTLE BITCH!" My jaw dropped. Selfish? **SELFISH?** I had given him everything he asked for, but just this once, I deny him—and this is the gratitude I get?

Geoff said he was taking me home. I cried all the way in the car—while he yelled at me. Then I thought, "Fuck sitting here listening to all this bullshit," about me being a "selfish greedy little bitch" because I wouldn't give him any more of MY money—that I had worked so hard to earn. I started to yell right back at him (not wanting to lose any more of my pride). Geoff pulled the car over, and told me to get out and walk home. We were miles from my house—at night—and I had no idea where I was, or how to get home.

So I refused to get out of the car. I buckled my seat belt to emphasize the fact that I would NOT be getting out, until I was safely in my own driveway. Geoff responded with more yelling—FEROCIOUS yelling. Then, being the gentleman he is, he got out of the car, walked over to the passenger side and opened my door screaming, **"IF YOU DON'T GET OUT, I'LL GET YOU OUT MYSELF!"**

I clenched my fists at my sides, ready to strike if he so much as touched me. I'll bet <u>he</u> <u>knew</u> not to touch me—because he didn't. He just stood there and kept screaming at me. I screamed back, telling him how I had given him virtually everything he had ever asked me for.

Geoff screamed at me the entire way home. By the time we arrived at my house my hysterical crying matched his screaming. I gave him $2 for gas money for taking me home. We didn't speak for a few days after that.

★

Dear Nobody,

Last night Vickie and I drove to Sam's house to wait for Geoff, planning to all go out together after he arrived. I figured it'd be a shade awkward, but guessed he and I would basically just ignore each other. My dreamlike optimism led me to hope Geoff might even apologize, or at the very least just be nice to me. <u>Dream on, Mary Rose!</u>

When he arrived (half an hour late), he started frantically screaming at me again. He even yelled at Vickie. He gave me the money he owed me—which was $5 short—and started screaming even louder when I mentioned that he had shorted me. Then, as we went to get into the car, he screamed at me and Vickie that we could not go with him and Sam. She was as shocked and appalled as I was, so we finally got in her car and left. We went back to my house and watched a movie.

After that I went to my grandparents for the weekend.

Now it's Monday and I haven't spoken to Vickie since Friday night, and she owes me $30. I hope to talk to her today. I have off today (and tomorrow). I was hoping she'd have off this afternoon too, but she's working till around four. I'll call her then to get my money and see if she wants to do anything.

☆

Dear Nobody,

Mom said Traci called me when I was in rehab. I haven't talked to her for a while. I should call her. Since getting back, I've been wanting to hang out with her again—even though there <u>has</u> been some drama—we are still pretty good friends. No matter what rumors are going around, I will always love her, because Traci knows all the worst shit about me, and she doesn't care.

Should I ask her what REALLY happened? Get HER side of the story?

It's probably just a rumor; but here's what I heard happened. I heard that while I was in rehab, Traci got drunk with Geoff— and she kissed him. I talked to Geoff about it, and he said he didn't do anything. He said he just ignored her. I don't really think he would have kissed her—she's the one who kissed him first. I just wonder if he kissed back or not? He says he didn't.

I'm not going to stop hanging out with Traci because of a stupid rumor, but maybe I should trust her as far as I could spit on her.

Oh, well.

This friend of mine, Pete, called Traci a Mary-Rose-Wannabe. Pete's really cool. We get along okay except his mom hates me—almost everyone's parents do. He's the sweetest guy that I know right now. Maybe if Geoff and I break up again, I'll ask Pete to the movies.

Geoff told me he was sick of us always arguing when we are together. I've punched him in the face during some arguments—but only when I'm drunk. It really hurts his feelings. Thankfully he's never hit me back, and never would. Since getting back together, I've stopped getting drunk enough to punch him, but we still argue a lot.

He can be really thoughtless.

Last night on the phone, he told me he wanted me to leave him alone and forget about him. He said that he didn't care either way if he ever saw or talked to me again. And that really, really hurt.

I wonder how he'd feel if I died tonight? Or tomorrow?

☆

Dear Nobody,

Man, I bet I know why Geoff acted so extra-mean the last time I talked to him. And I have a feeling that Vickie may have played a big part in it, too. See I talked shit about Geoff to Vickie, and Vickie must have told Sam, and Sam must have told Geoff. I know Vickie can't stand me. She's really only nice to me when she needs money. She's a real miserable bitch when she doesn't need anything. It's just that I don't have anyone else to hang out with, except for maybe a few other girls that I could start to chill with (they don't just USE me, or treat me like SHIT).

Well, I'll have to get my money back before I ask Vickie if she told Sam to tell Geoff everything I said.

FUCK THEM!

I don't even really care all that much anymore. If they want to be my real friends, they'll prove themselves, as I've tried to for them. Loyalty is all I really want. Those kids aren't even much fun (but we all need someone to pal around with). I hate that fact.

Well, I only worked one day this week. I caught some sort of stomach virus and have been puking my ass out for the past two days. I feel better, but not completely. I'm supposed to go to some party tonight. Ha—a drinking party—my stomach will LOVE that. Anyway, tomorrow is Halloween, so after I go to this party tonight with this one girl, I'll probably do something tomorrow night with another girl, and maybe the girl from tonight.

Well, I smell and look like shit, so I have to go take a shower and all that shit. Tomorrow I have to get some of my shit back from this one girl, pick up my paycheck, and then I have to get my thirty bucks back from Vickie.

Dammit, man.

I've got so much shit to do, but I'm so fucking bored.

Dear Nobody,

Geoff won't talk to me.

I hate that time during fights between "friends" when nothing has been resolved yet, and it's too soon to find out if anything can be reconciled. Especially when it's one of those fights that could mean "The End." You see, I've noticed that my different friends get into fights for different reasons. That's why we've all (most of us) got back-up friends—to keep us occupied during the intervals between the spats with our "real" friends.

Even so, the time between is SO BORING. Maybe that's even the reason why WE DO reconcile—the feeling of knowing that right now we could be out, doing something worthwhile, something we'd like to do—but instead are driven out of desperation to spend time with these alternative people. This desperation is what drives us back to our old "friends"—clad with apologies and nervous smiles—no one wanting to come across as being grandiose, yet no one even conceiving the idea of being too humble. That is a far worse travesty than losing the friend (which is why it all started in the first place).

And different friends have different battles, and different "calming periods" that come after these battles. For example, alcoholic "friends" usually stop talking for a day or two, to weeks, sometimes because of things said or done while sloppy drunk. Sometimes over fist fights. Usually these differences are made up by the next time a person wants to get drunk, and has no drinking partner.

Then of course there's always getting extremely drunk and calling from a payphone covered with the stench of liquor and vomit on our shoes, pouring our heart (and apologies) out.

Potheads just forget these altercations. Which is ironic because usually they can go the longest without talking to who they used to, simply because potheads will smoke a joint with just about anybody, anywhere.

Coke-heads are always fighting, or arguing, yet move in and out of conversations so quickly that it's almost barely noticeable. They do have their problems too, but usually money is at the root of it.

Heroin is a weird one. It means so many different things to different people. The people that use it usually not only need it, but also need some of the people that come along with it. It's not really something you can do continuously all by yourself. You almost always need other people to keep it going.

Either way, whatever group, drug, fight, or grudge, I hate the waiting in between. It SUCKS!

☆

Dear Nobody,

I haven't talked to Geoff, my stupid ex-boyfriend, in like two weeks and I'm glad. I'm much better off without him. But right now I've got a hickey on my neck—and I'm not sure who it's from—and I don't care, either! I did 69 with Sam, who I really like, but he's not my boyfriend—we really only talk when we're drunk. His friend Pete and I make out, too. I really like Sam, but I'm loud and obnoxious when I'm drunk and he's very withdrawn—kinda quiet. Sometimes his responses to what I say feel fake, or like, heartless and thoughtless; I dunno, maybe he just doesn't know what to say. He's social, but has anti-social habits. I heard him say he doesn't care about anyone but himself.

FUCK THAT—I want to change that so bad!

I really like him—but there's no way I'm going out with him and then have him hating and lying about me like everyone else. He's too special.

☆

Dear Nobody,

Hooray! Hooray! I got Geoff to forgive me! He called, and we talked a while—him being solemn, and I being the one doing most of the talking. I had no idea that our argument had hurt him THAT much—it was almost touching. Then he said shit, like, how he could never forgive me for what I had said, that it was completely over for us two forever. He said he'd never been so angry in his life—and it kind of made me glad (in a sick kind of way)—that I'd meant enough to him to hurt him so badly. But then when he started saying all that "It's-definitely-over-bullshit" I began to panic. I apologized. I expressed my shame and humility and owned-up to the destruction of our relationship.

He was a tough cookie about it, but I broke out with some of my best shit, although I was feeling a shade Pinocchio. I'm glad it was over the phone, because I had a big smile on my face for some of it. I'm not sure why; maybe because it struck me odd to hear myself saying these things—almost begging his forgiveness.

After maybe an hour of such shit, he said he had to go.

I said for him to at least think over what I had said, that I really did not mean any of the horrible things I had said before, and that he had absolutely every right to be very mad at me— but, **"PLEASE, PLEASE DON'T LET IT RUIN WHAT WE HAVE! DON'T LET IT RUIN US!"**

Well, after feeling like a criminal, or a liar on a witch trial, he said he'd call me back a little later. And he did—to see if I wanted to go out.

Hmm—never forgive to forgiven in fifty-five minutes flat. Shall I be an actress or a lawyer?

I was ecstatic at his change of "heart." Thrilled. He picked me up an hour afterward. The night started tense, but by the end—we were gazing at each other with more romance and tenderness than Romeo & Juliet.

Yep, I worked a little bit of my magic, hee, hee, hee!

I'm just irresistible.

☆

Dear Nobody,

When Geoff forgave me, instead of deeming him as a sucker, instead of losing all respect for him and denouncing him as a weak excuse of a man—quite the opposite happened. I was genuinely touched by his forgiveness of me. It made me feel more human in some way—more special; and not in an obligated, indispensable way, but in an emotionally gratifying way.

I'm so glad to be back in my baby's arms. Yep, maybe I could love this one—he makes me feel so special—and he has restored my faith in the awesome power of forgiveness. It's just such a beautiful concept; and now Geoff's beginning to seem more beautiful, more real, and all the more wonderful to me.

I could maybe love him. I am almost there. I also know he has to care for me a great deal. I said such terrible things to him and he granted me forgiveness—after only a little anger and a little hurt was expressed—it should have been in exchange for much more anger and hurt, yet he spared me that unpleasantness. What a man. Then after all of that, there he was, welcoming me back with open arms. It felt so good.

I'll remember this the next time somebody really needs my forgiveness.

Dear Nobody,

So, me, Geoff, Sam and Sam's twelve year-old brother, Fred, went to the cemetery to get fucked-up. We each had two forty-ounce bottles of Crazy Horse Malt Liquor. We all just sat in a circle under the full moon on the soft grass—seeing who could get their first forty down the fastest. I remember the forty-ounce being extra fizzy that night, probably because of the cold. Sam finished his beer first—as usual. Even though Geoff is older than all of us—as well as the biggest—he threw-up first (mostly fizz). Fred ended up puking right afterwards, but he finished second, which was my usual place. Then I finished. Needless to say, with 80 ounces of malt liquor pumping through my hundred and six pound body, I was pretty drunk—and loving it.

We were all getting dizzy and Sam wandered over to a tall tree and started to piss. Geoff got up to talk to him—and started spinning in circles while describing, to no one in particular, how dizzy he was. Fred just sat on a tombstone grinning at Geoff. Then they got up and walked over to the tree. I tried to get up, but I toppled over—which was fine by me because I got to lie on my back and look at the sky. Even though the trees were shading the cemetery it was extremely clear that night. The stars were almost unnoticeable compared to the bright, shining moon. It almost didn't look real. I wondered if I was the only person in the world looking up at the beautiful sky that night. I glanced over at the three drunken clowns I was with, and wished that I was somewhere else.

Sam and I were probably the most intoxicated (as usual). He came over to get me up, and by then I had started a conversation with the vomit lying beside me. I apologized to the vomit for cutting our conversation short, before stumbling along after Sam. Geoff and Fred were ahead of us. Soon we established a new residence near the cemetery exit. We sat and talked for a while—happy with our new location—until we saw two police cars parked at the cemetery exit. Four policemen aimed their flashlights in our direction and started to walk toward us.

Geoff and Fred jumped up and ran back into the cemetery. Sam probably could have escaped too, but looked after me instead. He tried carrying me—but we both just spilled-over after the first two steps. Sam ran and hid from view behind the gate. He motioned with his arms for me to follow him. Intoxicated me thought if I ran fast enough—between the two cop cars—that they'd never see me. I immediately took off running but didn't happen to notice the step I had just skipped. I flew to the ground—landing between the two cars.

The cops didn't notice me until I hissed at Sam asking for his location. The two cops walked around the car and I heard Sam's voice telling me to run. I got up and immediately fell. I got up again—and started running as fast as I could. Just when I thought I was going to make it—one of the cops came up from behind me and shoved me onto the ground with both of his hands.

Next thing I knew I was on the ground licking gravel off of my lips. A flashlight shone directly into my eyes—not only was I dumbfounded—but blinded. I let out a guttural wail as I felt the cop's knee further compressing my back, as he put handcuffs on me. The cuffs were so tight they pinched the flesh on my wrists. The officer got one more good weight shift on my ribcage before his codependent came and they pulled me off the ground by my hair.

They were asking me questions just as fast as I was blocking them out. They pushed me in back of the cop car and I hit my head—hard—on the door frame. I flinched, after trying to use my elbows to stabilize myself, and realized that my elbows had been turned into puddles of pus and blood—and that the palms of my hands were raw and filled with bits of gravel. I screamed again when the cop pulled me upright. Blood was dripping from my arms and my calves and staining my socks.

The policeman said they'd loosen the cuffs if I answered their questions.

I agreed.

They asked me if I had been drinking or doing drugs.

I shook my head, "No," thinking it was partly true because he'd asked about drugs, too. As I shook my head, I felt it fall to my shoulder. I just left it there.

The cop said I smelled like liquor and asked if I was intoxicated? I told them, "Yes."

I sat in the cop car for a long time. No one had loosened my cuffs yet—and sweat poured into my wounds. The saltiness stung, and the smell was making my stomach turn. I could see gravel in my knees and feel it on my palms and elbows. I looked over to the other car and saw Sam with his face down on the ground. Two cops were on top of him. He was put in a different car than me.

A cop finally came back over to me and loosened my cuffs. He got in the cruiser on the driver's seat and pulled out of the cemetery. He didn't say anything to me, which is kind of unusual (but I am in no way complaining) as we drove. I let my head hit the window with a thud and listened to his radio crackle and the dispatcher routinely spit out codes—of domestic disputes and auto theft.

The cop said he was taking me straight home, instead of to the station—which I was thankful for. We were almost at my street, when I hear the dispatcher say a name I knew, "Dylan." I focused hard to understand what she was saying between crackles in the radio. When I heard his name, I started laughing; he was a really good friend of mine. My best friend. I probably would have been with him that night, if only he had answered his phone.

It was about two in the morning at this point. I was still buzzing from the liquor, and I started laughing at the idea of seeing Dylan at the police station. I wondered what he did to have the cops come to his house at this hour?

The dispatcher spoke in more codes, and then repeated his name. Then I heard her request an ambulance for him—due to a possible overdose. At first, I didn't believe it, but when I heard her say it again, I burst into tears and started crying. I was saying over and over, in between sobs, "No, no, I don't believe it!" The cop asked me what was wrong and I told him I knew that guy.

When we got to my house, I was in hysterics. The cop helped me to the door and explained to my mom that I was drunk and was found in the cemetery with a group of boys. I sat in a chair listening to my mother and the cop talking in the doorway. I yelled to my mom about what I had heard over the dispatch radio and she looked over at me. Then the cop looked at my mom and asked if she knew anything about it.

It turned out—Dylan had overdosed. He must have run out of the house as soon as someone had discovered what he did. My mother said Dylan showed up at our house around 1:00 a.m., with no shoes and no shirt on. My mom gave him a shirt to wear and talked to him for a while. She noticed there was something wrong with him and asked him about it. Dylan told her that he had overdosed on his Prozac—and other medicines. She talked to him for a while—then he left.

Not knowing I was there, Dylan went to the cemetery. He had to walk through it to get to the quarry, a wooded area completely isolated at night. Dylan went to the quarry—and laid himself out to die. When the ambulance picked him up, they found a bottle of fifty mg Prozac and bunch of heart pills and cocaine in his system. Dylan was in a coma for a while—and then his heart stopped.

<u>Something or someone can be torn from you so fast.</u> They can just completely vanish—before you even know it. My time with Dylan seems like it was all a dream. I can't help asking myself, **"WHY DIDN'T I HELP HIM?"** I tried; I FELT for him. I tried to be indifferent—and I think maybe he knew. All in all, I felt ultimately powerless. The effect of a friends suicide

is so confusing; a mixture of loss and guilt. I guess I learned from it too, though. I guess I learned to appreciate people more now. So that just in case, I won't have to appreciate them more when they're gone.

A few weeks before Dylan died he and I were in my basement hanging out. He was telling me about a dream he had where it was judgment day. He said skulls were flying around in the sky and he was surrounded by lightning. He said no one would help him—not even me. Dylan said in the end, everything was destroyed—<u>and he woke up screaming.</u>

Dear Nobody,

It's been a few weeks since Dylan's suicide and I'm still not over it. Geoff has been a dick about it. He can't deal with me when I "get like this." We got into another huge fight and haven't talked in a while. Just what I need.

☆

Dear Nobody,

Man, I haven't written in this damn thing for a while. So, everything's getting like VERY complicated now. I'll put it this way. I've been doing a lot of drinking lately. A lot. More than I've ever done, <u>AND THAT'S A LOT!</u>

Plus (I WAS BUZZING WHEN I WROTE THIS), I was drunk in public. I got arrested all of the times, except for once. So I have a $165 fine that will probably have to be paid by me doing community service. My hands, knees, and elbows are all torn up from when that cop pushed me down while I was running from him in the cemetery. Then he fucking held me down and put cuffs that were way too tight on me.

I forget how many times I've been cuffed since then....

☆

Dear Nobody,

Geoff called last night to apologize about Dylan. His words surprised me—and so did the gentleness of his voice. Hearing his voice was like hearing a song that you once thought was so beautiful and special that when you hear it again, you forget why you ever stopped listening to it in the first place.

I still remember. Maybe I always will.

As beautiful as that song was—it made me cry. It saddened me beyond belief; the melody of his tune always changes—its either deception, insult, apology, or a declaration of love.

Geoff's voice still haunts me—a song I can't quite recall all of the words to—stuck playing in my head.

Dear Nobody,

I am so happy right now. I am <u>in love.</u> Geoff makes me so happy—I smile and don't even know it. My heart beats and skips when I think of him. My stomach rises and falls whenever I see him. My legs weaken and my breath leaves when I speak to him. He makes my beauty even more beautiful—my spirit even more spiritual.

This feeling is MUCH MORE than just a feeling. He has put his entrancing spell of fascination on me. He creates even brighter and better dreams for me than the ones I thought before were so vibrant and big. I am lost in an indulgence of ecstatic joy and virtual bliss. Reality has no effect on me—he has become the only object of my reality.

And the sex is getting better. I wouldn't say he is a "sex god" or anything—but he IS improving. Last night, we did it on my mom's couch. He kept saying, "No, I don't want to," but I talked him into it. He finished after like fifteen-seconds. I told him next time it would have to be longer—or I wouldn't let him use my phone to call his mom for a ride home.

The next morning my mom came into the living room, wakes me up bitching and asking why my underwear's on the floor and the back door is open? What a HYPOCRITE! It's not like I haven't heard her and Joe doing it before. Like mother—like daughter.

✠

Dear Nobody,

Geoff and I are finally getting good at this whole "sex thing."
Sex is so exhilarating! Who knew? Every time is like the most
spectacular feeling! It pushes me in and out of consciousness,
taking me at first to new galaxies; then dimensions—until I feel
like I'm in TOTAL OBLIVION! Not like a void—but in a
place where my elation is so prominent it becomes even more
tangible than the physical aspects.

I think the key to evolution is in sex.

I can become anything or anyone during it.

And it's not even the sex that dumbfounds me—it's the
orgasm part. It's like my body was made with a built-in pharmacy
between my legs. During sex, I am higher, more vulnerable,
more excited, nervous and more relaxed—than any chemical
drug has ever made me. During sex an indescribable rush happens
to me and elation takes me—I am under its control. It pushes
me to a level of consciousness that could easily be mistaken for
unconsciousness. It enslaves my mind and body. It feels like I am
in a trance that will confuse me later; but I'm so emotionally and
physically expedited that I don't care WHY I feel it—I just care
THAT I feel it. It's like a misty, fragile sort of depiction.

Human words could not describe the places I have visited.

I feel like me and Geoff are the only two people ever to visit
this universe we created—and since we created it as one—we
become the only organism in this new universe.

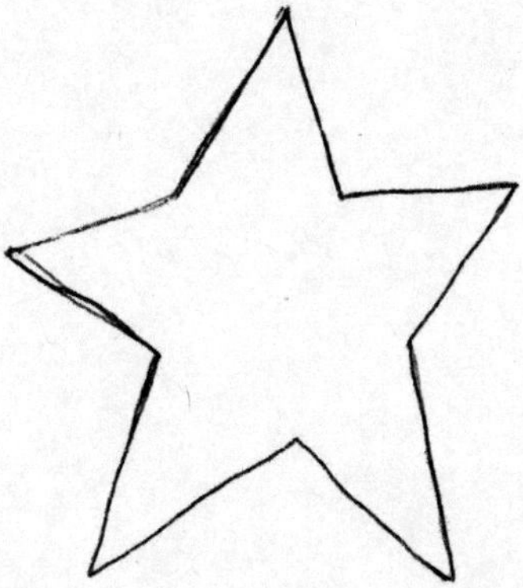

PHOENIXVILLE, PA
WINTER, 1997–1998

Dear Nobody,

I've been getting really sick again; probably because of all the drinking. I was forced to go back to school. Almost none of the kids there know I'm sick. So I just stomp around school, looking like a fucking rag.

Since getting sick again, I've become one of the palest people there—and I have black hair now, so I kind of stand-out next to those pretty, blonde, tall cheerleaders. I'm not as tall as everyone else and I'm only ninety-seven pounds right now. My legs and hips have been hurting like hell lately, too—so I slouch and limp a little when I walk.

I've been getting this loud, chronic cough lately—and everyone turns to look, and roll their eyes, and say a lot of stupid shit about me. Yesterday, I was standing in the lobby at school and started having this nasty coughing spell. Sometimes when I'm at school I just try to swallow that vile shit I cough up—or hold it in my mouth until I get to a bathroom. But by then I'm REALLY sick—the taste is awful!

I really didn't care what the people standing there thought—I just walked in between this big group of jocks standing by the trash and spit this big-ass wad of green, bloody, chunky phlegm in the trash can. They all cringed—and told me how "attractive" and "ladylike" I was, and some other shit I'm trying to forget. Since like third grade certain people have called me "Germ" for doing shit like that. Now if I'm at school (and I don't care who is around) I just spit on the floor. They thought I was repulsive before? I'll SHOW them repulsive. Mucus doesn't (besides the taste) gross me out. I mean shit, how could it? My body is practically made of the stuff.

Sometimes, I wonder if they would say these awful things if they knew it was because **I'M SICK?**

Probably.

It wouldn't matter to those assholes.

★

Dear Nobody,

Tonight it's Christmas Eve—I'm running around the house wrestling with my sister, we even danced for a while and I was singing almost all night. It was great! Then I chased her through the kitchen and into the living room. On my way into the living room I jumped over the couch and flipped—so I was hanging from it upside down. I was making faces at her—and then I started coughing.

I thought it was mucus. So I yelled for Nicole to get me some Kleenex to spit into. There was tissue paper lying right there on the floor from a gift I opened earlier, so Nicole handed me that. I spit into it; it didn't taste like normal mucus. I looked in the tissue paper to see if it was a different color. And it was— bright red. Pure blood. No mucus even. Just blood. All of the sudden—just like that. And my chest didn't even hurt. I started to scream—not from fear or anything like that, but from anger. Just ANGER! I'd never spit up pure blood before. It didn't scare me or hurt me or anything. <u>It pissed me off.</u>

I mean, here I was on Christmas Eve, having so much fun that I hadn't had for the longest time, and then something like that happens. Something to remind me that my fun won't last and that it only gets worse from here. Why? What did I ever do? Why am I spitting bright red blood up, in mouthfuls, from my poor lungs? While my eight-year-old sister watches me and my mom runs into the room?

I'm so young, I'm too young for this shit, but I feel like I'm getting too old for it, too.

I was in the hospital for three days and when I finally got out, before I left, the doctor told me that when I was first admitted—he thought I was going to die. So for Christmas I got something special that none of the other kids in my neighborhood got—and it came gift-wrapped in tissue paper.

☆

Dear Nobody,

I went to see my doctor and guess what? My lung function was 108%! That's like a normal set of lungs! My doctor couldn't believe it—neither could anyone—to have your lungs go from working only 30 percent then up to 108% is VERY unlikely. It gave me kind of an invincible, immortal feeling—I had forgotten what it was like to walk more than twenty feet without losing my breath. Like, "Yeah! See everyone? Not even chronic illness and lung disease can stop me!"

But then, on the weekend, I slipped up really bad.

<u>All I'm going to say is that I was really not concerned with my health at the time.</u> And when I do something like this, when I slip up, no one understands how I could do it.

Well, the only explanation I can think of is that after I've been feeling so healthy and normal, I kind of stop worrying about my health—because I start to have that invincible-like complex. And believe me, I thank God for it every day; but every time I destroy my health, it seems I get it back.

But now, because of this weekend I just had, my breath is a little shorter, my mucus is dark green to brown and a lot thicker. And now I've got this chest pain that keeps getting worse and worse, and this pain in my hip. My mom is calling the doctor again...

☆

Children's Clinic
of **Philadelphia®**

Dear Hayley,

Hello Angel, how are you? I'm very sorry I haven't written to you for a while, but I've been in this goddamn hospital. I've got a PICC line in my arm—which is like an IV, except it goes from my arm (a little tube) to my heart. It pumps in this medicine. I also have to do a lot of those breathing treatments—two every four hours. As soon as I finally get to sleep there's five people in my room waking me up for another goddamn breathing treatment. At least I don't FEEL sick.

Remember how before I said I was so lonely? Well, I think that I was lonely then so that it would prepare me (a little) for the loneliness I have in here. I was only supposed to stay for one week, now they say two.

I'm going nuts because this place IS fucking nuts. The people here are either liars or bitches (or both). My mom can only visit me on weekends because she has to work. Sam and Traci might come up to see me soon (I hope).

This hospital is a clinic. It's about forty-five minutes from my house. I really fucking hate it here. Geoff calls me long distance as much as he can. Sorry if my writing is shaky, but I'm trying to do a treatment at the same time.

So, how's your Saturday night?

Man, it gets so fucking BORING in here. I don't have a

Children's Clinic
of Philadelphia®

roommate any more. I could go walk around looking at all the signs on the walls trying to learn Spanish. I'd only learn words like ELEVATOR, STAIRS, FIRE and BATHROOM though. Maybe I could just hang around the Psych Ward and learn words like PROTECTION FROM ABUSE, RESTRAINING ORDER, HOSPITAL BILL, and ABUSE COUNSELING.

Okay, I'm finished now. So do you like this card? I bought it at the gift shop downstairs then got bitched out for not being back on time (bitches or liars). Isn't she pretty? She's a little angle just like you and me. No, I meant <u>angel</u> not <u>angle</u>—I always confuse it! I like her hair.

Oh, I dyed my hair again. It's black. I'll send you more pictures soon so you can see it.

Well, I'm going to stop writing now and go make a sandwich.

Love forever, XOXO,
Mary Rose

P.S. Oh, don't pay any attention to the back of this envelope. The hospital tutor is trying to teach me how to do multiplication tables. I made it all the way to the eights! Always reckoned I was a smart bitch!

171

Children's Clinic
of Philadelphia®

Dear Nobody,

My real dad came to visit me in the hospital. He's in Reading, but he doesn't want me to tell anyone that he's here, because then he'll have to pay more child support.

Once when I was eleven, he tried to get to know me long enough until he convinced my mom to drop charges on child support for me. He gave me some song and dance about getting a new job close to our house and how it would allow him to be more of a "dad" and buy us presents and stuff. After my mom dropped the charges—I didn't see him for two years. Then, the next time I saw him, we had a sort of a "falling out."

And here I am fifteen years old—keeping a secret so he doesn't have to pay support. <u>I'm so stupid.</u> And he asked me if I wanted to move in with him when I got out—so HE can get child support from my mom! That's just bullshit. But I still put up with it—I don't really know what to do.

I just don't need him in my life right now—although I'm so desperate for company, I should count my blessings that I, at least, got a visitor.

Dad is scared I'll get drunk, and tell my mom that he's here. <u>I should just fucking tell her anyway.</u>

★

Dear Nobody,

I've been home from the hospital for a week, and I just finished reading letters from people I used to know and love, and looking over some old pictures. Then, to make things even worse, I found a tape of myself talking to three or four old friends of mine from Reading.

I sounded so different then, like another person, with another soul. I was talking, I was laughing, I was HAPPY. It was weird—to hear all of those old voices, to see photos of all those old familiar faces. Back then I seemed so carefree, and I was. I had so many good stories, a new one for every day of the week. Life was so great then, compared to now. It seemed like I actually HAD <u>FUN</u>. Now it seems like I just have a GOOD time, not exactly a FUN time.

I really, really, really miss FUN.

When will I start having FUN again?

☆

Dear Nobody,

My friend from the hospital died today. Her name was Jennifer—and like me, she had Cystic Fibrosis, too. Jennifer looked just as healthy as me. Our chronic cough was even the same (when I was coughing up blood). We looked the same—we both looked exceptionally healthy. Who's next? Which one of us?

Jennifer is not my first friend who has died. Tiffany was eleven when she died. Jennifer was thirteen. Heidi died before I even got to know her. Sarah is practically dead, but not yet. What about the rest of us? When do we die? We're getting old for our age. Sarah is seventeen at the end of October. She's in her old age. Timmy is seventeen. He's in his old age. Jess and Tiffany never got theirs. My old age. What is it?

Maybe Jennifer died instead of me?

After someone is dead and gone—especially someone so young, and beautiful—what I am supposed to feel—is not exactly what I do feel. When I had first heard Jennifer had died, I was in shock. I admired her beauty, her humor, and her intelligence. She had only been thirteen. I felt so many different ways all at once. I didn't know if I felt guilty to be alive, or happy that it wasn't me. I can picture her sitting right across from me—eight feet apart—which was the rule at the hospital—so that we didn't make each other sicker. We would smile at each other in between wheezes, gasps and coughs. Jennifer had befriended me. Talking with her was like having a conversation with myself; that's how alike we were.

Now, when I think of Jennifer, I picture her in a coffin. I see her big, caring eyes—sewn shut. I see her in a white dress, a very pretty one, and her arms crossed over her chest. I see the shiny gloss in her dark straight brown hair illuminated by the fluorescent lights we once sat under. But Jennifer seemed so ALIVE. It's hard to think of her body rotting in coffin. She was rotting when she was alive. So am I. We have been rotting from the time of conception. Disease, infection, swallowed her from inside out. But we are more than just a disease, we have souls. Jennifer had a soul. I wonder where it is?

I hope that her soul can read this.

★

Dear Jennifer, Tiffany and Heidi—and all the other angels taken too soon by Cystic Fibrosis,

You are all with me every minute of every hour of everyday. Every minute without you is a minute without air, gravity and life. You are rarely absent from my mind, and if ever you are absent, for the briefest moment, my mind drains into a pit of loneliness and torture.

No misery is as haunting and ravaging as your absence. You are so much more than my security and protection from this evasive earth. We exist in a place other than this disgraceful world of maddening confusion and tenacious hatred. We've got our own heaven that awaits us. We can only enter into it through our arm's perennial embrace of one other. Yet this dark world has sealed our only true home off from us. At least you and I know our way home. You have gone to our heaven first.

Will you wait for me? Will you shine for me up there as brilliantly as you shone for me on earth? I will look for you when I get there. I will look for your burning porch light that will guide me home.

Rest in Peace.

Dear Nobody,

I am seventeen. I'm OLD. I'm old. I look great for my age. Very good. I am living my old age. When you were sixteen, how many of your friends did you watch die? Did you know maybe one person that died? One friend? Guess what? I could count my dead friends on my hands. Guess how it feels to have all of your friends being wiped out and slowly dying off by the same Cystic Fibrosis I have?

God never intended this hurt for me. Please, please what did I ever do? Help me. Help them. Help us. Help us, we're in hell! No one can save us. Not our machines even. Not our pills. Not even all our endless, lonely hospital nights.

Help us.

Why are you healthy and all of us dying?

☆

Dear Nobody,

Jennifer's death brought up issues I can't handle—I JUST CAN'T
DO THIS ANYMORE. Sometimes it hits me—something like
this will trigger it and I will become scared to death. I still cannot
believe that I could be cursed with such a horror; to everyone
else, this is all second-person. I feel my limitations—my mortal-
ity. I will never know what it's like to be old, to have children,
to be married. Just like Jennifer, I'll be dead soon. The average
life expectancy for my type of disease is thirty two years old—
and that's if you take care of yourself, which I never do.

If I were being chased by a murderer with an axe, a knife,
a gun, bare hands, whatever—I could run, I could fight back,
and I could call for help. Now, imagine the panic and fear
you would feel in that situation. For that second—those few
minutes; imagine having that fear all the time, not being able to
get away from it; never being able to escape it.

With Cystic Fibrosis it's different. You cannot run from
Cystic Fibrosis. Fighting back at Cystic Fibrosis with treatments
and hospitalizations is all-consuming—and in most cases—
futile. If you can take the treatment tube out of your mouth
long enough to call for help, the only ones who can hear you
are either too ill to respond, or already dead. Besides, doctors
and nurses and social workers separate us freaks from each other
(they SAY it's for our own best interest).

Oh shit. How can I keep on doing this? This IV in my arm,
the pills in my mouth, the mist in my eyes—this ache in my
body? How can I do it any longer?

Yesterday on TV somebody said, "How can you fall in love with somebody that's got one foot in the grave?"

Who will want me?

Who will love me?

★

Dear Nobody,

My whole life, while other kids were trying to memorize frivolous things like codes to video games, or their time tables—I was trying to remember how many cubic centimeters per syringe to draw up and from which solution.

While other kids were learning how to play basketball or football, I was learning that if you mix Resulin with insulin and then hang upside down while getting pounded on it worked better to loosen the mucus. Strangers in uniforms would come and hang me upside down to help drainage, and pound me for an hour—four times a day—until it hurt to inhale. The harder the person hit me, the better the chances of me coughing were. And coughing is my greatest defense against this disease. And coughing was hell. My muscles and ribcage would hurt for weeks afterwards, and I often got headaches from being upside down.

I remember once telling one of those strangers that they were hitting me too hard, and they told me to stop whining.

So when other kids were getting snuggled by their parents, I was getting beat by some stranger, while my parents were miles away. I could never explain with just words how I feel about that, but it hurts. Back then, I wondered what I did to deserve this? Now I just wince and accept it.

Dear Nobody,

The first time I went into the hospital felt like my funeral. People sent flowers, prayed and visited; but over the years it seems that no one visits or sends flowers or cards. The last time I was in the hospital, the only get well card I got was from my school bus driver. My aunts, uncles, friends—anyone I thought cared for me—did not do so much as call. So I was pretty sad to say that the only get well card was from my bus driver. And I appreciated it greatly, knowing her concern and get-well tidings would soon fade.

I guess it's easy to forget the dead as time goes by. But I am not dead; this mind still THINKS, and these feelings still FEEL.

Dear Nobody,

Cause you've hung me upside down
Now I've lost my princess crown
But just ignore me if I start to cry
Cause if you don't, I'll probably die.

Dear Nobody,

I remember once when I was in the hospital—I was like twelve or thirteen—and there was this younger "CF" boy named Timmy on my floor. We talked about a lot of things together; from chest Physical Therapy—to PICC lines—to people making fun of us for coughing. One night, after taking all of our laxatives, foul-tasting syrups, antacids and pills, we ordered food from some pizza place. We got a large pizza and cheese fries. I borrowed some of his enzymes before we ate, and together we finished the entire order! Afterwards, both of our stomachs got extremely big; too big for our underweight bodies. Then we talked about that. Then more things about CF. It was sad, and later I cried for him, and then for myself. But I felt a little better; a little less like a freak.

Dear Nobody,

Today some guy at the gas station asked me if I was losing my voice, I said, "No." So then he called me a FREAK!

Why?

Because I notice the little pleasantries that are normally overlooked? Because of my interest in literature? Because of my physical imperfections? I am tired of having no one else around like me—and I'm tired of being called a FREAK!

Dear Nobody,

Tonight I'm going to talk about what a FREAK I am.

People call me that all the time.

Mary Rose is a FREAK.

Whenever someone calls me that I think, <u>if only they knew.</u>

Someone called me that yesterday and for the first time, after years of being called it, I finally FELT it. The words finally affected me. I was at home doing my treatments and as I was sinking the needle into my arm I wasn't thinking about the pain, or how I have to take twenty pills after this and then give myself another shot—instead I was thinking... freak? FREAK?

I could show them a real fucking freak, if that's what they want. I could hold out my arms and show them my scarred, torn veins from the many PICC lines and needles that have been in me. I could point out the big scars—the long, thick marks the IVs make when they fall out of your arm. They could just look at my hands closely and see how FREAKY I really am. Instead of judging me on my hair or my clothes. Instead of whispering to each other about my thin body and my bony face. Instead of flipping their eyelids up in judgment when they see my black nail polish and skull rings. Instead of looking just past me, beyond me at something in their hindsight, they could look at me, INTO me and see something REALLY worth talking about.

They could talk about my little white scars and all the red marks, scabs and bruises that I have on both hands. They could point out the big fat vein—the one on my left hand—the one

185

that is so scarred and ruined that it sticks-out like a tendon on a thirty-two pound anorexic. Maybe if they looked at my fingertips, they'd notice the little red and white scars all over the tips, and they could whisper about THAT. Maybe they'd see the blood blisters, or the way my fingers quiver when it's cold; or get hot because of nerve damage.

They could REALLY get into how FREAKY I am if they looked at my legs closely and noticed how one is a little bit longer than the other, because my hip started to fall apart and dislocate when I was ten (on its very own, how fucking freaky is that?!?) Maybe me and those fucking assholes can take a little trip back in time—and they could see me when my joints were so fucked up that I had to be in a wheelchair for two months.

Maybe I could invite them into my house at around eight at night and they could see me swallow my twenty-five enzyme capsule pills all at once. Yes. I can swallow TWENTY-FIVE medium sized pills at once, without any water. And I've been able to do it since I was nine years old. How many people do you know who can do that? Hmmm? Guess that would **MAKE ME A FREAK, huh?**

Maybe I could just show them my counter full of medicine— THIRTEEN different varieties—that are ALL for me. Then I could show them the basement with its boxes full of more medicine for me. Oh wait, what's in that fridge there? More medicine for Mary Rose?

"Gee, like, oh-my-God, that's A LOT of medicine."

Then maybe they could put a math test in front of me and see how well I do on it, because, at the moment, I wouldn't do very well at any test. "Mary Rose must be stupid," they would think, looking at my low test scores. Well, maybe you would be stupid too if you hadn't been well enough to attend a full school-year since you were in second grade. I missed weeks—months even, because of my illness. How come I'm not as bright as my classmates? Gee, THEY all seem to know what they're doing. But me? What am I doing? I don't know what I'm doing—maybe my brain is not clear because I'm too busy concentrating on the tiny fact I'm dying from an illness that I didn't ask for, or deserve.

Oh-my-God, you're right! **I AM A FREAK!** Guess that makes me different.

Okay wait, what if I could take them into my living room and show them the three big, loud machines that "keep me breathing"?

Do you have big loud machines in your living room that keep you breathing?

No? Didn't think so.

Oh, wait, I've got them! How about if next time I sweat I show them how salt crystals form on my skin? REAL salt crystals, that in the sun look like glitter all over me. Or I could let them check my blood sugar. Maybe it'd be 600. Would yours?

Wait, I know how I could show them freak—I could eat something, wait a few minutes, and let them see what happens to my stomach—let them see how big it gets. Maybe they'd think I'm just pregnant, but I'd tell them the truth. I'd tell them it was because <u>I can't digest my food.</u> Nope, my stomach won't digest my food. How about your stomach? Will it digest your food for you?

Or I could let those bastards listen to me choke on my coughs. I mean REAL coughs—ones that hurt. Ones that hurt right before they come, and even more afterwards. Ones that make you think you'll never breathe again. Yeah, do you think then, they'd really think I'm just a little more of a freak than they thought I was?

I could even cut myself open and try to show them my gene mutations. That's right. Mutations.

As in **MUTANT.**

Dear Nobody,

Sometimes I feel like being the biggest bitch alive. I feel like being as completely heartless as possible. I want to send shivers down people's spines and turn their stomachs. I want to desensitize everyone's heart with my indifference. I want to return everything that everyone's left in my doleful path. Not only will they know the hurt, shame, embarrassment and loneliness they've taught me—but at least this way they shall FEEL it, too.

☆

Dear Nobody,

I'm not going to lie. Right now I feel very drunk. I already apologized for being drunk to Geoff.

I told him about my Cystic Fibrosis.

He started talking about his Dad who died.

He told me he never visits his grave.

I told him I didn't want to hear about death anymore, and hung up on him.

Oh shit, I see the word death—that means DEATH.

I'm sorry, I love you...

Hello Nobody,

Right now I am drunk. Not too much. Not drunk on love, or pain, but alcohol. Which is both. I shall die if I am to be without it. I am so drunk—therefore truly numb, but I feel my emotions now. The void called love, the misery called shame, and the hurt called pain. I am an alcoholic to a sickly extent— and an addict to a fatal extent. I was born of a sickly gene pool and un-blissful intelligence. My only comforts are my darling acid tears—AND ALCOHOL.

☆

Dear Nobody,

It's 2:23 a.m. on a Sunday. I can't sleep. I feel kind of raped.

Yesterday Geoff told me about how this guy fucked me after I passed out. It's my fault. If I didn't drink and pass out, that wouldn't have happened. I feel so dirty and empty.

When you're a slut, you feel like THAT'S ALL you're good for.

See, this feeling is different. It's a cross of anger, and some other unexplainable feeling; just one more thing to humiliate me. What can I do? I put myself in this situation.

If I told my mom about this, and how I feel, she would just say I asked for it. So I have no one to talk to about this. Geoff is my only friend; I hate everyone else—but I can't talk to Geoff about this.

I'm so pissed. How could this happen to me? It's my fault, I guess. I mean, I've been taken advantage of before, but this feels different—I was UNCONSCIOUS. Maybe I have no right to feel the way I do? What the fuck can I say about this? I can't even remember it. I can't. I hate males—FUCK THEM!

Geoff is the only one of those fuckers I still care about.

Shit, I feel so fucking empty. No one to trust, or talk to either. It's all my fault. Man, I can't explain this feeling. I want it to leave. I feel empty. I just feel like being alone. You get what you deserve.

I apologize to myself—but I can't forgive myself.

☆

Dear Nobody,

Geoff and I are finally done. Yeah, it's all over. I feel like a glass of spilt sherry. On the phone he said he wants Vickie, or her friend Michelle, instead of me. I basically called him an overweight fuck-up. I told him that he'll never get laid unless he started losing weight, ESPECIALLY by me.

Geoff asked me if that was a promise.

I said it was his loss.

He said no, it was his gain.

I told him that his fat ass need not gain anymore of anything.

Then old Geoff had the audacity to make a hot dog joke about me that's too hurtful to repeat.

I was so humiliated and hurt—the thought that the love of my life, the bearer of my heart, my first true love, the most respectable man in my life had made a hot dog joke—it was the worst thing he ever could have said. It symbolized everything I hated people for—and he had gone and done it. He had made me feel exploited, violated, and humiliated—just like everyone else.

We haven't spoken for over ten days. It's a record.

Yes, this is it. I'm done with him. I'll find someone better. Can't say the same for him.

He was basically a nice guy.

Oh, well, I know he can't forget me. Two nights ago, he called and hung up—until 3:00 in the morning. All calls from payphones.

I must be costing him a fortune in quarters.

193

Dear Nobody,

Last night I was out walking around after me and mom got into a fight—when I saw some of my ex-boyfriend's friends walking toward me on the opposite side of the street. They called me over and asked me if I knew where Geoff was.

I was like, "How the fuck would I know?"

While we are all talking—I saw Geoff come out of a house right by us—then he quickly went back in when he saw me. I called his name and he came back out on the porch. Standing behind him was this girl he's been seeing (I guess it's his new girlfriend). He had her initials tattooed onto his chest. I was just like, "Oh, so this is how it is now?"

At first I didn't say anything. Then I began calling his name. He just looked at me with a really nasty expression on his face. I asked him to come down and talk with me, but he refused. All of his friends just stared at me like I was a dumb-ass. He said how yesterday I acted like a bitch. Finally I just walked off. I was really kind of embarrassed and pissed. I felt pretty humiliated. (What a surprise—ME? Humiliated?)

Later, I ran into his friends again and tagged along with them. We all went to search for alcohol. Some cute hippy dude with a car saw us outside the liquor store, trying to buy some and he got it for us. Then we got into his car and went to the cemetery and got drunk. It was a lot of fun. Then we went back to his house and he invited some of his friends over. Man, he had some hot friends. I passed out and spent the night at one of their houses. It was a cool night—but I'll probably never see that hippy dude again. He lives in Hanover or some shit.

But at least I didn't think about Geoff all night.

Dear Nobody,

I feel so betrayed and used. But what the fuck else is new? I'm lonely. I can't trust anyone at all. I guess I'd better get used to it. Man, for almost six months I trusted and cared for these people. I lost and sacrificed a lot for them. I really loved my friends. I had let them become almost my life. And what have they done to make me feel so betrayed, empty, and lonely?

One raped me while I was passed out. I heard if the girl gives no consent, or can't, it's rape. I really trusted him, too. The other motherfucker (or maybe it was all those motherfuckers) broke into my house and stole three fucking CDs (one of them was fucking Nirvana, too) AND they stole the VCR. The next fuck-up lied to me very badly and abused my trust.

Fuck them ALL. At least until I find a different form of assholes to suck me dry and leave me all alone. Now this pile of books are my only friends for a while.

I don't know, I just do this sometimes. I'll lose everything and everyone, but then as soon as one little shard of something or someone to grab onto floats by me, I grab onto it as if it'll save me from getting sucked under and drowning.

I'm almost sure that that's what brought me into my last mess. I don't need any more messes for now.

But I guess I'll hold my breath—<u>and walk right into the next one.</u>

Dear Nobody,

I have never felt worse. I'm getting a little sick again, and Geoff is being a dick. He's just purposely trying to hurt me. Just like everybody else. With the rape, I am feeling a little bit better now. As far as other shit (drugs and alcohol), it's getting to me again, and I really can't let that happen. That shit fucked me up enough already.

Now Phoenixville High School wants to send me to residential rehab. RESIDENTIAL. Yeah, you fucking live there for however long—like I haven't been away from home enough. Fucking shit, I just got out of the goddamn hospital two weeks ago. The people at my school say they want me to go because my mom is an alcoholic in denial, and even though I haven't drank for a while, her drinking could trigger mine. Yeah, but aren't they going to fucking send me right back to her anyway? They say if I get help, maybe she will get help. Why the fuck do I have to be her fucking martyr? And she's been fucking MEAN to me this week, like worse than ever before. So why the fuck?

The insurance company might not pay for it. I am hoping to God they won't. And now she wants me to go see her parents. I swear I can't fucking stand that goddamn place. I'll probably fucking end up killing myself or something. No fucking way I'm going.

Fuck them and that.

Fuck It All.

Oh, and now they want to put me in fucking Special Ed.

because of the school I missed. Kiss my diseased ass I'll be in Special Ed! I'm not fucking Stupid!

FUCK THAT!

Oh, yeah, and I also have to go fucking under anesthesia because my stomach is bleeding. They have to do a test. Yep. Some kind of goddamn ulcer.

Gee, I wonder what the fuck that could be from?

FUCK IT ALL!!!

☆

Dear Nobody,

All of my friends—even my ex-boyfriend—deserted me tonight. I got really wasted—and I begged them to take care of me while I was fucked up, but not one of those assholes did. They were all lying and shit to get me away from them—because I was falling around on my ass and being loud.

Geoff just completely forgot about me. And I know why, too. I have my period—so he can't get any. Otherwise he would have probably just fucked me and let me pass out, but instead he just completely forgot about me.

The party broke up; all my friends left and I had nowhere to go. It was horrible. So I was just like, "Fuck it," and I went back to the broken-up party and begged them to let me in and crash. They were already pissed at me and hated me for making noise.

They told me, "GET THE FUCK AWAY, YOU UGLY BITCH!"

So then I got even more pissed and told them I was staying on their porch that night.

One guy was like, "We'll let you in if you suck our dicks!"

The other one was like, "Hell, no, I ain't letting that bitch near my dick!"

I wouldn't have done it anyway.

Then one of the fuckers pissed on me. Literally.

I told them to give me some money to call someone and I'd leave. They gave me a dollar in quarters and I left. I felt like shit. I was out of tears by then, and my knee was bleeding from when I fell earlier. I walked toward the payphone at Turkey Hill gas station to call Geoff, beg his forgiveness, and ask him to come and get me.

On the way over there, some guy around thirty-seven or forty-years-old asked me to get into his car. He started calling to me from across the street and I couldn't see who it was. I thought maybe it was one of the people from the party who felt bad—and were gonna give me a ride, so I walked over to him. It was some man that I'd never seen before in my life—so I ran away from his car as fast as I could!

I had walked about halfway home, when my mom's car pulled up next to me and I got in. Apparently a "friend" of mine had called her and told her that I was smoking weed and drinking and was walking home alone in the dark.

Yeah, tonight SUCKED!

★

Dear Nobody,

I only fuck the ones I love...
So why can't I love everyone?
Everyone seems to love me...
Because they're always trying to fuck w/ me

☆

Dear Hayley,

Gosh I wish we were talking in person. It's been SO LONG. I miss you more than anything. No one else seems to understand things from my point of view. People take advantage of me, spit on me, and rob me when I'm out. After a while I just don't care.

I start waking up in houses I don't know, with people I don't know—with roaches and dry puke everywhere. Winter is the worst time too, because I can't just sleep in a park or alley; it's too cold. And when I'm drunk I do stupider things; like sleep in crack houses full of perverts and weirdos who are just waiting for me to pass out.

I miss Geoff sometimes, but things were so fucked up. I just HAVE TO keep on remembering that part.

Well, Hayley, write to me when you can. Remember I love you and that you are my **best** and only real friend in this world. Take care.

I♡U! TONS! I MISS YOU! TONS! Love you, MaryRose

Dear Nobody,

Geoff's friends know me better than he does. I know alcohol better than I know him. Geoff only loves me when he's drunk. I'm still in love with him, but so what? Love is supposed to be reciprocated. This love is ruining me. I need to get rid of my love for Geoff. He's killing me. He's doing the worst thing he possibly could to me—HE'S IGNORING ME!

☆

PHOENIXVILLE, PA
SPRING, 1998

Dear Nobody,

I haven't seen Geoff in three torturous weeks and counting, a lifetime emotionally. My angel. My better half—no, my whole. My everything, my all. Even my health has never meant as much to me as he does. He helped me with my pain more than any narcotic ever had—and he's caused me more pain then my condition ever has.

If I ever see him again, I will pluck out my own eyes, so that he is the last thing that I see.

If I ever hear his beautiful voice again, I will puncture my eardrums and make sure it's the last sound I ever hear.

If I ever touch him again, I will offer up my body up to the Lord. I would trade his touch for the most horrifying leprosy.

I want his touch to be the last thing I ever feel.

I want to carry a part of him inside myself. I wish I could become impregnated by him and offer it up to God in a painful miscarriage, if only to have the chance to have his bloodline in my meek body. I would give up everything for the chance to have a part of him growing inside of me, even if it would inevitably perish.

My darling, my amazing and beautiful savior, I would speak the three most powerful words I know: <u>I love you.</u>

Then I would cut out my tongue and offer it up to God as yet another plea to be the last words ever heard from my mouth. And while I am lying somewhere a deaf, infertile, mutilated, blind leper—I wouldn't wish any of it back.

Not for a second.

☆

Dear Nobody,

It happened again last night. I just keep slowly fucking up my life. Every weekend it gets worse and worse. The shit just piles up. It's like I'm drowning and have nothing to grab onto—because everything else is sinking, too. It's like I never mean to fuck up so bad, it just happens.

I was arrested again last night. I was out past curfew and trespassing. It was cold out and I had a skirt on, and no coat. I had a coat earlier that night, but it got stolen. While I was in this place trespassing, the owner came running out. We all ran, but I was behind everyone and didn't see where they went. It was raining and freezing. I lost my (favorite) shoes and had to keep running. I ran an entire mile home with no shoes and no coat; soaking wet from the rain. What's weird is that—I couldn't feel the sleety rain beating down on me—and I couldn't feel the cold—or the small sharp rocks under my feet—as I ran. It's like I was numb. I didn't even run out of breath or energy—I just kept running. I liked how my shadow looked laying on the street and the noise my feet made splashing through puddles. I thought everything was going to be okay and that I had escaped. Then I saw the cop car ahead of me and heard the cop call my name. I was almost home, too—I probably would have made it if only I hadn't stopped running. But stupid me, I stopped, and got arrested for the however many-ith time.

It was five in the morning at the station when my mom was called to come pick me up. She was obviously pissed, and I was inevitably ashamed and humiliated, once again. Even though I hate her right now, I STILL feel bad for letting her down.

I got a letter in the mail today saying I owe like $400 for fines by April. Or else, they said, they would have to take further action...

☆

Dear Sum-body,

They were taking the batteries out from the remotes (in case I tried to hit them with it). They all talked in complete codes, purposely played that video game.

Everything I saw was sex of devil-like stuff.

Eating a cookie was awesome. So was drinking Gatorade.

It turned to daytime after being under a lot of trees for a while.

Paranoia kicked in, I wondered what they were doing in the front seat. Kept seeing (three boys at a Uni-mart, one girl maybe eleven years or older) and a skateboard.

Everyone positioned; standing right to make a perfect abduction, back-up plan and all.

Like prostitution, only all you get to do is look.

Crack whores pounding on the door.

Sixteen year old guy that's Mac and sells weed.

Everyone is sinister, up to something.

The sky looked cool.

Snakeman.

Snake, man.

Rocks came up from the ground.

He was showing him which moves to make—and how—and when.

Dear Nobody,

~~The day after I was gang-raped,~~ I woke up alone. I lay still on the mattress, pretending to be one of its many stains. A fluorescent blue light was coming in through the window and it poured over my body like an evaporated pool of calm—with deepness too thick to feel, only strong enough to sense. Was I laughing or crying? It was too dark in the room to check my reflection in the cracked mirror—I'm the last person I wanted to see right then anyway.

I wanted to move. I HAD to move, but could not. The loose spring stabbed at me through the mattress's worn, dingy cloth. I could feel it in the small of my back. Jabbing at me—poking me with its sharpness; scratching me with its dullness. I felt it under me; trying to bond me to it, trying to attach us—make us connect somehow.

It's only a spring.

ONLY A SPRING?

Maybe it isn't pulling me to it—maybe it's trying to repel me? Trying to make me leave? Maybe it knows that I don't belong here? That this isn't me? That this isn't my home? Maybe that spring knows that those guys could have killed me? Killed me, like a roach. The thought crossed my mind a hundred times. Probably crossed their minds, too.

The mattress is still damp with sweat.

Is this really as it seems?

How did this happen?

Shut up, spring, I feel you.

Abandoned Houses and Worn Out Shoes
on a weeknight

Dear Nobody,

Rape is by far the most degrading, disgusting, horrifying, depraved act of humanity ever invented. No words can describe the sheer terror of the rape's moments. Moments that last for hours. Hours that turn to days. Days that turn into a lifetime. And the terror, it never leaves. NOT EVER. Oh, it diminishes some, but only to make room for the paranoia—severe, chronic paranoia, the kind that stays with you—behind you—in front of you—ready to reach up from your own shadow and drag you with it back into the darkness—back into the worst part of fear—to the unknown.

Dear Nobody,

Panic—I am taken back to that time, to a place that I never knew existed, until those boys took me and gang-raped me—and left me there. It's a panic attack that rushes through my body, completely uninvited, just how THEY came—completely uninvited. As the taste swells in my throat, I go into shock.

Did those boys over there say, "HOLD HER," or did they say "OLDER?" Are they really talking about football, or ME? Why did they just look at each other like that?

I'm losing control. I sense what it means to walk into a room, and immediately take caution to where every man in the room is at all times. It's paying more attention to dialogue, and listening closely for any hidden meaning or code. It means never stepping too far away from the nearest exit, in case I'll need to run. It means looking around the room for anything to use as a weapon. From remote controls to firepokers to telephones, I keep my eye on them at all times. It's sitting on a single chair, instead of a couch. It's watching for sudden movements in everyone.

It can't happen again. It CAN'T happen again. I tense up. I can't breathe. Do they know I know? I'll act like I don't know, so they won't hurt me or kill me.

If it happens again, I'll kill myself.

Why? Why did I ever go there? I KNEW it. It's all MY FAULT.

I should have NEVER left the house.

Dear Nobody,

I really wish I could get amnesia and forget everyone and everything that has happened to me. I'm starting to wonder what I'm good for...

I don't have low self-esteem, but I think I can be a horrible person—bossy or selfish. I guess I am, because all the times I've been anything different, I still get the same results—only with a little less respect. What's going on? I never imagined it would turn out like this, but then I KNEW it all along. I wonder if in heaven I can forget my past?

I can't believe how horrible and worthless I've gotten to be. The only way to hide it is to act over-proud and be grandiose. At least then I can pretend, but I wonder how I keep going on like this? I don't even know if heaven could make me happy. On a talk show I heard a renowned psychic say, "It doesn't get any worse than this" (meaning life after death), <u>but does it get any better?</u>

Maybe it's like a test, and I'm Job from the Bible or something? Can I ever really be happy? I just want to completely forget who I've been and who I've known.

Dear Nobody,

Am I as different as I think I am? Am I as different as I feel? I've tried, but I cannot explain my exploration of the dark alleys and shadows—the more dangerous, the better. I'm never sure of just what it is I'm looking for, but I always find something—from rapists to rape victims, I find them all. What's so unintelligible to me <u>is that I don't fear any of it.</u> Yes, instinct finds me when I sense the person behind me walking too close for comfort, but instead of avoiding the situation, I sought it out by just going there. Does that make it my fault? No, I don't ask for trouble, but I also don't deny it my time and chance.

Maybe it's just that I'm searching in all of the wrong places for what I may possibly never attain? But exactly what I'm looking for is a mystery even to myself. In a word I could say "more" but as to more of what—I am completely oblivious. But isn't it better to drink <u>dirty water</u> than <u>thirst</u> to death?

Morality Drug
Cry Dark Empty Fear Jesus Wary
Pain Terror Tears Blame
Help **RAPE** Anguish Alone Loss Death Trustless Power Defenseless Sting
Sickened Body Violence
Loneliness GOD Anger Me Abandoned Diselusion DIRTY
Lost Scared Paranoia Rip
Scream Hurt Ruined Damaged Heal Trapped Wrecked Broken
Disbelief
Alcohol

217

Dear Nobody,

I'll think that I am ugly
And blame it on the media
I'll kill myself and blame the legends
We all die at 13 anyway
I'll get raped and blame myself
We've all been raped before anyway
I'll think that I could never fit in
And blame it on the other kids
I'll be an alcoholic
And blame it on my past
I'll have fat thighs and blame it on my mother
I'll abuse my kids and blame it on my father
I'll steal a watch from Walmart
And blame it on my income
I'll never learn to read
And blame it on A.D.D.
I'll never tell anybody I love you
And then blame it on them for not telling me
I'll become a racist, and blame it on an incident
I'll go and do something very stupid
And I'll blame it all on my youth
I'll be an American
And I'll blame it on America.

Dear Geoff,

Geoff, do you feel ANYTHING for me? Please don't ever let me know if it's just physical—I'd be so humiliated.

Geoff—do you think I'm crazy? Everyone else does; I don't know if I care though. But it's so humiliating. I use that word a lot. HUMILIATING—I feel that a lot.

Am I stupid, Geoff? I really feel like it, but I'm not sure. I'm always fucking everything up for myself. Other people sometimes help, but it really all starts with ME. And I can't help it. I won't blame myself, because I really don't try to be stupid. Actually, I remember you calling me stupid. We were both drunk. You called me a stupid bitch and I punched you. You got really pissed and I said sorry over and over again, until I finally started breaking shit and you accepted my apology—probably so I would stop breaking things. I humiliated myself that night.

Geoff, what do you really think about me? Maybe someday I'll just humiliate myself too much and just let you know how I really am on the inside. I tried to that night I told you about my "condition." That memory still humiliates me—everyday. Maybe if I knew you loved me, I wouldn't feel humiliated all the time. Because I love you—but you already know that.

Love forever,
Mary Rose

Dear Nobody,

It rained all day today. The rain can be so sad. Maybe it's all of those times that I refused to cry, or couldn't cry, coming back to me. The whole world's tears that have never been cried; and all the clouds look like tears yet to come. The storm is supposed to move on by tonight—I hope I can do the same. At least Traci knows about my disease—and about me getting raped—and doesn't judge me or think it's my fault.

☆

PHOENIXVILLE, PA
SUMMER, 1998

Dear Nobody,

I'm so bored. I'm so confused. My life is still so empty. No friends, bad dreams, no life. I'm going to try to get a job as a hostess at some restaurant, or maybe at this nursing home. I'm only gonna work where other kids are working, so maybe I can meet some people to maybe be my friend or pass time with at least or something.

I don't want to be friends with anybody from this stupid, mean town. Nobody here relates to me. Nobody here is even anything like people I'm used to being around. I hate it. I'm so sad here. My life feels so lonely and pointless.

After I study for my GED (diploma) my mom says I can go to college this fall. I hope so. Maybe even this summer I could go to college in Atlantic City and live at my grandparents house. I don't know. I just hate being lonely. It hurts, it sucks, it's sad, it's scary, it's DANGEROUS. I feel so miserable. Here I am, missing the friends I had—the life I had. I want a way back to that. A lot of people have lives. Why can't I?

I dropped out of school. That's where everybody meets their friends. I have no high school friends. I have no good memories. Nothing. I'm sick of it. It makes me want dangerous, bad things. Drugs—hard drugs—and people who are bad for me, but I don't care, because I'm so lonely and no matter what their intentions are at least they're talking to me…

✗

Dear Nobody,

I woke up today to the sounds of locusts and birds. I stretch my legs out and arch my back and feel that ache that's always there after a night like the last. There are no sheets on the mattress—but dry vomit is lying right next to me. I must have woken up earlier and threw up. At least it's already dry. I scratch some of the puke off the bed, and then roll over to face the wall. I can't sleep any more.

I get up out of bed, close my window and walk downstairs without looking in the mirror. I'm exhausted. I go into the bathroom and piss for what feels like fifteen minutes straight. Man, I'm thirsty. I'd kill for a soda. Caffeine would get me to feel better. My mouth feels like cotton and booze. I walk into the kitchen and stumble into the refrigerator—unable to walk straight. Maybe I'm still buzzing but my balance has been off lately. I put a pitcher of juice to my dry lips and gag. The scent of that sweetness nauseates me and reminds me of the sickly sweetness of the peach flavored vodka I had been drinking the night before. There's no milk, so I guess I'll have to drink water. I'll mix it with Strawberry Quick. I've got to get this taste out of my mouth. There's already pink powder all over the counter. I must have made it last night, too.

I look in the mirror before walking out the door. My hair is tangled and sticking to my face. There's vomit crust in some of it. My face is puffy and my eyes are swollen. There's eye make-up on my cheeks and eyes. It's smeared. I do the best I can to wipe it off with my fingers. My hands are kind of shaky.

I feel weak. Oh shit I'm getting nauseous. I run to the bathroom and throw up. The scent and sound make me feel even sicker. I sit on the edge of the bathtub, unsure of if I'm finished puking or not. There's already vomit all over my tee shirt. I've been wearing this shirt for three days now. My pants are dirty and a little too big—I think I've lost weight. Oh shit, here it comes—there's the sound of it splashing into the toilet. I feel a wave of vomit rise up in my throat again. Some splatters up on my face. After it's all out, I sit on the floor and drool on myself because I don't want to swallow any of this taste in my mouth.

My head hurts. I think I banged my elbow on something. Fuck I can't wait to get drunk. It's around eleven. People will be on their lunch break—they'll get it for me. I'll get a 40 because I only have three dollars left.

It's hot and sunny outside. I walk down the block. I'm sweaty and smell sweet like alcohol. My mouth is dry. Shit I feel gross, so full of toxins. I don't have my shoes on and my socks are getting dirty, but I sort of like the way the little stones feel under my feet. My feet are sort of numb but that's okay—I can't feel them blistering from the hot pavement.

Why am I here?

Why am I DOING this?

Dear Nobody,

I hate this town, I hate these morbid people, and most of all, and worst of all—I am beginning to hate myself. I'd have never even thought such a thing (let alone write it) back when I had friends.

I hate being this lonely. It's dangerous. No one is here for me, ever. I am alone. I come alone, and I go alone. I was born alone, and I'll probably die alone...

☆

Dear Nobody,

Oh God, I miss Dylan. Almost eight months later, the loss of my best friend still makes me cry. I think I probably started to drink so much because Dylan is gone. Dylan was like my drug. He made me happy no matter how sad I was. He could always get me to laugh. We completely understood each other. We were each other's family when our real ones weren't there. He was not only my best friend, but my only true friend. I loved him so much; like a brother I grew up with. I admired him profusely more than any person I've ever known. He was that kind of friend I saw being around forever—his kids playing with my kids.

Once I had a dream he came back and saw me. It was so wonderful. But then I woke up, in this lonely room, back into my lonely life and realized he's gone. Oh God help me, I miss my Dylan—please send him back to me!

☆

Dear Nobody,

My life has become a dormant haze of boredom and bad hygiene. Day in and tedious day out, I am stuck in the same hole that I've dug for myself—out of my own apathy. Every morning before I open my eyes to face another day in the bland and ill-fated world of being a fucked up junkie girl in America, I take a few minutes of my soon to be wasted day to imagine the places I COULD be waking up—from whorehouses to boarding schools; from a rain forest in Brazil to a desolate igloo in Antarctica—I've imagined them all. But paintings and drawings are all I'll probably ever know of these lands I dream of.

Is it my fault that I may never see these places, these preoccupying dreamlands of mine? Or have I seen them already, merely by pondering their existence? Do I exist in the land I live upon now, even though I cease to wonder about its existence? No, this land I live on now does not exist because I don't believe in it. Maybe that's why I think of it as such drudgery to be here.

I am comfortable in my boredom—I prefer it to my misery. While those other worlds may offer excitement and energy they may also offer pain and grievance. For now I'll have to be content with this world I'm in now.

But I'll still dream…

Dear Nobody,

I HATE MY LIFE.

I mean that more than I've ever meant it before. I realize it could be worse, but I also realize that it could be much, much better. Matter of fact, it was, once, a long time ago, and ever since then it's been decaying way past the point of "okay," or "just bearable."

Now it's blistering and intolerably painful.

I have NOTHING. Absolutely nothing.

No love, no hate—no passion. I have no education, not even a high school diploma. I've got absolutely no friends. Not even a best one. I am so LONELY.

It's terrible. I feel so close to hell.

I haven't even got my health. It's always half-way there—taunting me with the possibility of a "real" life—yet always ready to remind me that illness is just around the corner.

Never compromising.

Never just letting me live, or just letting me die.

I am always shackled in-between.

☆

231

Dear Nobody,

I have to say that while last summer was bad—it was heaven compared to this one. Last summer I was just getting into partying and all of that. In the winter, it got to be about more than just partying too much. I NEEDED to drink. I started smoking crack and doing coke frequently. Actually I did anything I could (Garbage Head). I was coming home drunk almost every night. In winter—after I was raped, I cut back a lot. I stopped using as much and only drank on the weekends—and my mom and probation officer never found out. In the spring, I began to cough blood again and began to use alcohol to numb the chest pain. After that incident in school—I stopped genuinely caring about anyone, except for my own self; if you couldn't get me fucked up then—FUCK YOU!

It only got worse this summer. I can't leave the house unless I'm tipsy—and when I do leave—it's to go get more liquor. I can always find someone who could buy for me. I don't think about anything else—except alcohol and drugs. As soon as I wake up, I drink—and won't not stop until I pass out for the night. I'm really skinny and pale. My eyes are always bloodshot and heavy. I have a big black eye and I always smell like alcohol. I have countless bruises. I've started to do things when I'm sober that normally I'd have only done if I was fucked up. I'm losing weight and look like shit… I think I'm gonna have to go back to rehab….

⭐

Excellence in Addiction Treatment™

WERNERSVILLE, PA
SUMMER 1998

CURON FOUNDATION

Excellence in Addiction Treatment™

Dear Nobody,

Ever since I've been in rehab, I keep having the most terrifying dreams about the guys who raped me. They always come at me—with the intent to kill me. I scream, I cry, I try to run, but I am stuck steadfast to the earth, my feet melting to the ground. I try to run—to fight back—but I am paralyzed. I see my Geoff and our friends looming around in the darkness; barely acknowledging what's going on. When my voice returns I scream out; I kick out violently with all of my might. I beg and plead for the rapist's mercy; I beg and plead for Geoff or ANYONE to rescue me, BUT NO ONE HELPS ME. I am brutalized, raped and put into the trunk of a white car. The rapist—followed by Geoff and his friends—get into the car. I'm left half-dead. Other times I fall while running—and wake up with a jump. These dreams feel so real; so frightening. The thing that hurts the most is that Geoff doesn't ever try to save me. I wonder why he hasn't returned any of my letters?

INVENTORY WORKSHEET

Sometimes I think it must have all happened by chance. Other times I am almost certain every second of my life has already been planned, and is waiting to be lived. I've had enough, haven't I? At first heroin was just for fun. Then I needed it. Mentally and physically. I felt sick without it sometimes. It seemed all that mattered. But how? How could it be? If it weren't for that one night, could my whole life be so different? If that one night never happened, oh, if only. Perhaps it was fate. Perhaps it was to be? Why? Why me? Hmm? It had to have been planned. Will things ever be any better? Dare I say as good as they were? I look around myself and wonder, "Who am I?" How could this ever have happened? And where's Mary Rose? Who am I? How could my life have gotten so screwed up? I've lost all happiness, and control of my life. How?

Excellence in Addiction Treatment™

Dear Geoff,

Hey, it's me again. I'm BACK in rehab! I keep writing to you, but you don't write me back. I miss you. I'm in pain right now and can't breathe too well. After they let me out of here I'll probably go straight back into the hospital—the one in Philly.

I've thought about you a lot while I've been in here; when I was a little girl—and then a little older—I always thought I'd only fall in love with someone from the hospital—someone like me. But, instead I got someone even better than anyone else—I got YOU.

Geoff, Geoff, GEOFF!

Oh Geoff, I wish you could have seen me when I was a lot younger and much more healthier. Then I wish you could have seen me when I was younger and much more sicker (in some aspects). I always daydream about if you could be there with me for all of it.

Maybe someday, if they give me a transplant or find a cure for me, maybe then you will stay with me.

I've just always thought that and thought maybe I should write to you about it.

Write soon.
XOXO,

Mary Rose

MY GEOFF, MY BEAUTIFUL, MYSTICAL GEOFF,

If only you could actually be here, pretending to ignore me when I know you need me to say what I am saying—right down to repeating your name a few times to pretend that I think you're not listening.

I like to say your name. Geoff. Sometimes when you're not here I'll say it, and hope that just saying it will make you think of me wherever you are.

Isn't this crazy? I'm writing you a fucking letter. Isn't that sad, Geoff? I LOVE YOU. There, could you hear that? No, you couldn't hear that, Geoff, because you're not here.

Shit, it's already four a.m. I wonder if you're still awake. Sometimes when I'm in lockup I stay up and listen to the bugs making noise, or pretend I have someone here (usually you) to talk to. And sometimes I just pretend I'm an actress and that I'm only in here so I can act it better for my next movie or play.

Might sound dumb, but they make us go to bed at 8:30, so I get REAL bored REAL fast. And sometimes I have to go like an hour earlier because I wouldn't clean the cum off the toilet, or wash trays or be quiet when we lined up for something. Yep, so I have lots of time to think about what other people are doing (like breaking into my house and getting fucked up without me).

Fuck those crackheads. I've got Traci. And my mom.

Actually I don't really care about friends when you and I were spending a lot of time to get her (well, not a lot, but more than just me begging you to come over at like 2:30 a.m. so you could leave in like an hour and a half). Remember the first summer we met I'd see you from like lunchtime until we got arrested (or went home)? That was a good summer. I saw you a lot then. And I still remember everything from when we first met.

Damn, Geoff, I could write a book. I can't believe that was like two years ago.

When I concentrate I feel like it's still happening. Or it feels like it was all just some dream.

I'm sorry all I'm doing is bitching—but all of it's true. My next letter will be more cheery, okay? I just really want you to know that I love you, and that I miss you terribly. Please take care of yourself. Please stay how you are. I love you forever. FOREVER. NO MATTER WHAT.

Love forever,
Mary Rose

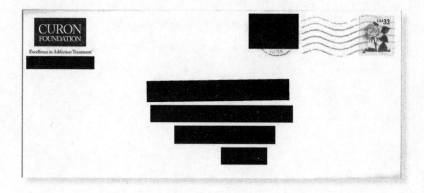

Excellence in Addiction Treatment™

Dear Geoff,

Why haven't you written me back?

    I love you because you are not beautiful. You are not perfect.

    I love everything in you—that would be destructive to love in myself.

                                                       XOXO,

                                                  Mary Rose

Dear Nobody,

I just got out of the rehab after being there for a month. More than a month actually—five goddamn weeks. Did anybody care? No. Did anybody visit me? No. Do you think anybody proved that they loved me? I think we know the answer to that—no one even responded to my letters. Five fucking weeks of hell. **HELL.** I know the word. I know the place. Rehab, hell; same fucking place.

After getting out I had to go into the hospital for a very painful surgery. My face is still bleeding from it and the Codeine they prescribed isn't helping me much. I could deal with the pain if I had help. If I had someone to take care of me. Geoff—the only one I ever loved or trusted—doesn't give a fuck about me anymore. He didn't visit or contact me once when I was away. I could care less.

It's my first night back home, and the slut bitch I call a mother won't even cook me a meal. Not to mention that right before my surgery, she showed up with Joe's fucking engagement ring on! They've made it "official." Why is she so stupid? Joe tried to kill us; and he would have killed us if the cops hadn't shown up. Now she is going to MARRY him?

I don't care about anything else right now—I just want some dinner.

Dear Everybody,

Jesus wouldn't even date my mother.

☆

Dear Nobody,

I think rehab may have worked. I know I can't drink anymore. And pot and crack destroy my lungs. But I've always just
needed to feel totally disoriented to forget about all this shit. It
was pot before my lungs got bad, then alcohol before I passed
out and got raped. What's left to do? If I'm gonna fucking kill
myself, I might as well die from drugs. I won't be missed. All I
need is to be totally loaded. Even just for a few hours would be
exceptional. I just need to get away from all of this. My hands
fucking shake so bad from nerves. Sometimes even my head or
legs. I just want to get loaded. I guess I'm gonna have to start
getting used to my sober self. God this SUCKS!

☆

Dear Nobody,

Mom kicked Joe out. She said she isn't going to marry him. She finally chose her kids over her stupid abusive boyfriends and I couldn't be happier.

☆

Dear Nobody,

My mom and I are getting along tons better. We are both significantly happier. People are just being nicer to me in general. I am healthy enough to be active and energetic—I never dreamed it could be so fun. I'll never take being able to run or ride a bike and keep my breath for granted. Everyone says that a cure is going to happen soon. I can't wait. Maybe I'll be cured by the time I'm eighteen. I hope to God.

Well, I'm just glad things are going well now. I hope they always stay as well.

PS: HA! What the fuck was I thinking! By eighteen? IF EVER!

☆

Dear Nobody,

Tonight at the mall I held a guinea pig. There was a cute one in a movie I saw with Nicole on Saturday, and I've been thinking of getting one ever since. (mom probably won't let me). Man, it's hot out. Wish I had a pool. Used to. At least I'm getting a tan, and maybe lightening my hair a little. I'm on this antibiotic that says to stay out of sunlight. Maybe that's why I've been so tired lately...

★

Dear Nobody,

Tonight I am supposed to go to the Lilith Fair with my mom. I don't know why I have reservations about going. It sounds like fun. Mom wants to go. I hope I get on TV. I'm going to jump in front of every camera I see. It's nice outside, so that's good. Our tickets are for the grass.

☆

Dear Nobody,

Okay, we went down to the Lilith Fair, and it ended up being sold out. I was in such a miserable mood. Seeing all those other girls with their friends made me sad. I don't have any friends. Not here. I felt miserable, and like a loser, and everything else people with no friends feel like. At least I had my mom. My mom and God.

☥

Hi Hayley!

I miss you, so I'm writing you a letter. I'm not sure just where to send this, but I'm pretty sure it'll find a way to you somehow. So how have you been? I went to the beach last weekend. New Jersey is doing okay I guess. I forgot to take any pictures, but tomorrow I'm going to some little party by this river so I'll try to take pictures for you there. It'll be prettier there probably anyway. They don't have woods in Arizona, so I'll send pictures with lots of trees and rocks. Do you ever miss those things? I never even noticed those things until I <u>really</u> looked at them.

Well, I haven't been doing all that much lately. I've kind of been in one of those moods where I should just stay in my house, because I feel like being alone, and I could probably hurt someone's feelings without even knowing it, IF they were talking to me that is.

A few days ago, I went to Philly to go to that Lilith Fair thing, but it was all sold out. Some guy came up to our car and gave us all these stickers. So I have these Lilith Fair stickers and nothing to do with them because we never got in, so I don't know if it sucks or not, and I can't believe we couldn't even find any scalpers there (even though we were like two hours late).

Well, I quit smoking that stupid weed shit. You see, I realized that lately before I go out, I've been smoking way too much stupid ass pot, so then when I go out to find other drugs, by the time I get there, I'm either like FUCK IT or I'm already high and keep forgetting who told me what, or where to go, or who to ask.

And pot is just not worth all that. Barely does much anyway. It's like cigarettes I guess. Like kindergarten shit.

I keep having these weird dreams. You were in one last night, with some old man. You weren't talking very much, but you were making me laugh. Are you doing okay? I mean, I know we can take care of ourselves more than anybody else can, but you seemed so sad in my dream. Like sad in a secret way. Like you didn't want anyone to notice. The old man was sad, but didn't care who noticed. You were almost going to follow him somewhere, but I asked you please not to. Do you have any idea what that could have meant? I'll have to think about it next time I'm tripping.

Hayley, what do you look like now? Please send me a picture. I'm going to send you some of me. I got my hair cut last winter, like short to my chin, but it's grown out some. Do you remember when you were showing me pictures of your old apartment and those people? You had a picture of this girl you said looked just like me! See, I know I'm just bringing up all these old things, but when I go into one of these just-stay-home-moods, I like to remember everything, and then think about it, kind of so I don't forget my life.

Man, I'm watching this stupid show on TV. I broke the VCR so there's no movies to watch. Oh yeah, I'm not drinking as much either, because I always end up breaking something. Not because I'm mad, just because I'm drunk. Like the other week I dropped the phone and it fell on the floor and the batteries fell out. Someone yelled, "Mary Rose broke the phone!" And then someone else yelled, "She didn't break the phone, I can fix it!" Then they got in some stupid fight over who was going to fix the phone, so I stomped on it a few times and said; "**Now** Mary Rose broke the phone!" I was laughing and just making a joke so everyone would shut up (it's hard to get drunk people to shut up) but it worked.

The next day I had to get a new phone, but it was my phone anyway. So that's why I'm not drinking like I used to (it's getting too expensive). Maybe I'll dye my hair again. Oh, I got this guy to buy me earrings. They're gold. These little gold kitties. I named them both Hayley. I never take them off.

I hope you'll call me soon. I lost your phone number. Sucks because I have a thirty minute phone card, too.

Well, I'm gonna go paint my nails. I love you! I love you! I love you!

~~I MISS YOU~~! I MISS YOU TONS!

XOXO Love,
Mary Rose

PHOENIXVILLE, PA
FALL, 1998

Dear Nobody,

I miss Geoff. His sweet smile, the cute things he'd say. I've never felt so close to anyone, or adored anyone as much as I do him. I miss his tangled curly dark tendrils that crowned his precious head, his beautiful dramatic dark brown eyes that shimmered like a river under moon light. I miss his brooding, but somehow proud posture, and deep way with words. Oh, I feel like a part of me has been taken far away, and now I'm incomplete. I've worn his blood and dried his tears.

I wonder if in heaven he will be my angel? Only in heaven will it be, when I could see him there, smiling again at me. To walk through the hell alone, to never have him there to hold my hand. How can I care for him so much when he has abandoned me in such hurtful ways? Is it really him I love, or the idea of loving him?

☆

Dear Nobody,

I'm starting to feel again. Even though it's in the wrong season for rebirth, I am starting to bloom again. I just want some fun. Some friends. REAL friends. I miss my old ones. I miss them so much. It still hurts. It's almost ruined me. I've narrowly escaped the dangers of my misery, but I'm not out of the storm yet. Sometimes I feel like I don't even want any more friends, then other times I feel like I'm desperate to hang out with ANYONE. My life is strange like that; I don't know if I'm lazy, or if I just want to put myself in hard-to-be-in circumstances? Maybe it's both. I don't know.

If I assume GOD will work everything out, he usually does (THANK YOU). I feel like if I try to stay half occupied until something happens, I'll be okay. I need to be content on my own for now—but I also need to remember my mom and Nicole, too. Mostly I need GOD. I just want to be satisfied.

Tomorrow I might try to call some theaters or something about acting lessons or work-shops or auditions. I tried before, but it was really cliquey. But I figure once they see my talent, they'll either envy me, or respect me—I'll either make friends or enemies. Worst comes to worst, I'll at least get to be acting.

☆

Dear Nobody,

I was just watching an interview with Gene Wilder, one of my favorite actors. When asked what to concentrate on while acting, he said to concentrate on nothing. Nada. Knowing he's a genius, I was heeding his every word. The more I thought about it, the more sense it made to me. Every day, in real life, how much are we really concentrating? In simple actions like having a conversation with a familiar face or in arguing with an unpleasant associate, how often do we look back and think of how we forgot to mention something—or of the perfect rebuttal to an argument? If we had been fully concentrated on the situation, we'd know what we wanted to say; what the perfect thing to do at that moment would have been. It's only later when we are really concentrating—by then our heads are clear—after we've gone over the situation in our mind a few more times. By then, we are not distracted by the heat of the moment, the shock of what the person is saying, or who that guy was that just walked by.

Dear Nobody,

I guess I really like to write. Maybe someday I'll be a writer. I've been writing lately just to write. I can't decide if it's because I like releasing thoughts from my cluttered head, or because I just like the way the pen feels gliding along the paper? They go together so well. Oh, and one thing about a boring life—you've got to stretch your imagination farther to come up with fiction, than if your living a busy, entertaining life. Busy lives have more inspiration. I guess, overall, a bored writer becomes the best writer, because they develop a more brilliant imagination; while the busy writer may only develop the skill of moving reality into fiction.

☆

Dear Nobody,

Today Geoff—that "ex-boyfriend" of mine—called me. We talked for a while. He broke up with that other girlfriend because she was saying really asshole-things. He says he wants to see me again. He said another PRETTY ASSHOLE THING, too. I'm not even going to get into all this shit though, because I'm kind of upset now.

Basically, guys just want pussy. Girls just want something or anything. It's not fair. Sexism pisses me off. I fucking hate it. Whenever a guy does something like burp really loud, I want to shove a tampon right in his fucking mouth. Like burping and shit is a guy thing. If a guy does it, he's being a guy, if a girl does it, she's being gross.

What really pisses me off is that a guy can fuck as many girls as he wants, and he's just considered a guy that gets it a lot. A girl that has a lot of sex is called a slut. If a girl sucks dick, she's usually called a "ho." If a guy eats pussy; he's just a guy that gets smooth pussy.

Double standards really suck.

Guys say that a girl gets loose if they have sex too much. I guess a girl CAN get loose just from doing it one or two times. Not even really loose, just not tight; but I don't know—is that really true?

⭐

Dear Nobody,

I went over to Geoff's house today. It was probably a terrible idea. After we talked, I walked home alone—smelling like him. The taste of him was still prominent in my mouth and throat. I almost liked it, in a self-derogatory way. It seems like anything having to do with Geoff is self-derogatory.

This isn't like me. I had always considered myself the extreme example of dignity—but not lately. However, if anyone were to say otherwise, I would deny it profusely. My failings and the personal fraudulence to my pride are very private, secret thoughts of mine. Sometimes I feel like I need them to keep my realities in check—other times I think they are the opposite, and keep me away from reality.

Like after tonight, I know what the chances of him calling are, but I dove into this head first, fully acknowledging the devastation I could be causing to my ego. It helps me to think of it that way—to think of MYSELF as the person causing the damage. It makes me feel less like the victim—I can still be the cement wall of emotional endurance—just so long as I can control it all.

See, I really don't CARE if he calls me.

I'm PLANNING on him not calling me.

Maybe.

Still, if he did—it'd be nice.

Hello?

Hello, reality, are you still there?

I think we've been disconnected.

☆

Dear Nobody,

Don't hate me—Geoff and I are back together again. I don't
know how long it will last this time and I'm pretending not
to care.

Dear Nobody,

Geoff and I are back together FOR NOW. I am desperately in love with him and he says he feels the same. I really fucked up my life this past summer. I'm gonna try picking up the pieces now. I want things to be calm and to keep getting calmer. However, my health keeps getting worse. I'm not sure I'm ready to anticipate my death anymore. I can't. I'm hoping they'll find a cure in my lifetime—they've already perfected cloning. They say that can help them cure me. I hope so.

Ø

Dear Nobody,

I knew I would be going back into the hospital soon, so Geoff
and I went down to the rope swing last night to try and get
my jollies while I still could. It was freezing out. I had on a big
winter coat and gloves. Some of the boys there had no coats
on, but I could tell they were freezing even if they were trying
not to show it. We were all in a big circle and I was sitting on a
dirty old box spring mattress that was lying on the ground near
the tree. There was a candle in the middle of our circle and two
cases of cheap beer. I held my beer in the gloved hand, because
it was so cold. I lent Geoff my other glove so he could hold his
beer because he didn't have any gloves on him.

When it got to be too cold to be outside we relocated
to an old abandoned house that is pretty far downtown; on
the East End almost. We kept drinking quickly because the
drunker we got, the less cold we'd be. A guy across from me
with no coat and a beanie hat pulled out a pack of generic
cigarettes and offered one to the guy next to him. He was
sitting on one of those old-people-plastic toilets. The girl
next to him was on a broken lawn chair. I didn't really know
the other two people next to her. Someone threw a piece of
ripped off cardboard from the beer case in the candle's flame.
It was starting to burn out. It was getting darker, and I could
barely make out anyone's face. No one was really talking—
just the guzzle of beer cans being drank in one gulp broke
the silence.

Someone else on the mattress lit her lighter to look for

cigarette butts by her feet. I could see a cloud of cold from her mouth when she breathed out.

This guy John burped really loud, and a few of the guys laughed.

The girl with brown hair said, "That's gross," then burped even louder; it almost sounded like she'd thrown up.

People were talking now, and it didn't seem so cold anymore. I was talking to the people on my left side, and they were looking at me, amused. The candle was just about burnt out when this cute Mexican kid stood up, looking a little happy, a little drunk; and said he was going to get another candle from the closet upstairs. Everyone just looked at him, no one really said anything. I stood up and said I'd go with him because he shouldn't have to go alone. I walked up the steps behind him. He was using his lighter as a flashlight.

We went into the bedroom and looked around. He didn't say anything, and neither did I. I walked over to the frosty window and looked out. It was snowing. He stood there looking around. I didn't like the silence, so I had to say something. "Find the candles yet?" I said, with too much faked concern, because I knew he already had.

"Yeah," he answered slowly.

"Okay, good," I said, and we started walking down stairs.

When we got back everyone was laughing, and passing around some ugly broken bowl with a devil face on it. Some guy had my glove on, and the girl who had been wearing it went someplace to pee. I sat down next to Geoff and kissed him on his cheek. I held his hand. It was cold; not as cold as

I thought it would be, but cold. Geoff was kind of staring off into the distance. It was getting quieter, but a few people were still talking. They were getting louder. I couldn't tell who was trashed and who was just drunk, but I had that feeling in my stomach I get when I'm pretty drunk.

The girl who had been sitting next to me came back into the room and flopped down on the floor next to the mattress looking listless. I asked her if she was okay. She didn't hear me, but I knew she was, so I turned my attention to the flame on the floor and listened to the other people talking. There were maybe six beers left from the second case, so I reached out and grabbed two and sat them behind me, while I finished the beer in my hand.

I heard one of the boys getting loud with another boy. I got into it, then the Spanish kid told us to shut up, that the neighbors would hear us if we kept arguing. We all forgot about it, and I kissed my boyfriend on the cheek one more time. He was really drunk—a lot of beer cans were at his feet.

"I love you," he said, hugging me.

I laughed and squeezed his arm. The Mexican and his brown haired girlfriend were looking at us, smiling.

✦

Children's Clinic
of **Philadelphia**®

WINTER, 1998–1999

CC®
Children's Clinic
of Philadelphia®

Dear Nobody,

I woke up this morning coughing up blood. I'm almost used to it by now. My lungs gushed bright red blood. It sputtered out of me. I choked on it. That horrible redness. It's like in the movies—bright, shocking red—the color of hell.

It's almost sick for me to say this, but I felt some RELIEF when I woke up with that distinct taste of blood in my mouth, because at least blood is thinner than that thick, chunky bile I usually cough up. At least with blood, I can swallow it before anyone sees. Unlike my death-stew that eats my lungs, the stuff that is too sticky and sickening to swallow. The mucus that gags and disgusts me.

I called for my mother and she called the doctor. When he arrived at my house, a half an hour later, I was still seeing blood on my napkin when I coughed. My mouth tasted like metal.

The doctor gave me two options; he said he could either put me in the hospital today, or try to make me better at home with strong antibiotic pills and steroids. I told him I wanted to try treating it at home—which we both know—NEVER works. The medicine he puts me on always temporarily turns me into an insulin-dependent diabetic, but it would be better than the hospital.

Children's Clinic
of Philadelphia®

Instead, they admitted me.

The doctor told me if I had waited one more day, I would have been dead.

☆

Children's Clinic
of Philadelphia®

Dear Nobody,

Tomorrow is Christmas Eve. I feel a lot better. My lungs are almost like a normal person's now. I want to stay this way forever. I'll still never be fully free from the illness, though. I have to take all of this medicine and do treatments. But at least I can breathe now. Although I'm happy to be feeling better, I could do without everyone lecturing me. The fucking doctors and social workers here need to mind their own fucking business about my personal happenings. I didn't come here for counseling—I came here to get rid of my pneumonia. They keep hinting that the reason I'm here is because I don't take care of myself.

That's the most bullshit I've heard about myself since the last time I went to school—taking care of my disease has become my fucking life!!! Who are they to say something like that? They are not there every fucking morning when I wake up and choke down thirteen pills, then do a breathing treatment and physical chest therapy. They are not there when ten hours later I take thirteen more pills and repeat the process.

Fuck them.

I really wish they could have my disease for <u>just one week.</u>
FUCK THOSE FUCKERS!

Children's Clinic
of Philadelphia®

Dear Nobody,

I've been in the hospital for three days. My lungs hurt from all the coughing. They are full of scar tissue and bleeding flesh—wounds from coughing and treatment.

Every day I try to walk through the halls of the hospital pretending not to know how bad things really are. Trying to smile. Trying to ignore how much it really hurts and how scared I really am. It's not hard to pretend; this has been my life since I was a baby. So much of my life has been taken away as I rot in hospitals, emergency rooms, doctors' offices; wearing this horrible loud vest that monitors my breathing.

Every day I walk around knowing that this horrible poison is in my body—growing in me like a cancer—eating my body like leprosy. And my family and friends treat me like I'm already dead.

I think of all the friends I've known, that have slowly died right before my eyes. I see people like me every few months, and sometimes—if it's been a while—I say to myself, "Damn, he's really starting to look horrible!"

Sometimes I'll think how awful and destructive sounding someone's cough has gotten. Or how much weight someone has lost. I'll notice that so-and-so's got more machines dragging behind them—barely keeping them half alive. I wonder if when people see me they think the same thing?

Children's Clinic
of Philadelphia®

Sometimes if I'm very, very sick and feel like I'm dying—I make it a point to gather all of my strength and stare at myself in the mirror. I've done this over the years and over the years the reflection that looks back at me has gotten more and more frightening.

Last night I saw my chalk-white pale skin; my grey chapped lips and my heavy teary eyes. The veins in my face looked ripped and bruised. My skin was so dry that it seemed translucent. My ribs could be seen plainly through my chest, even without me sucking in. Somehow the oxygen tubes seemed to have taken up my entire face—overpowering all of my features.

☆

Children's Clinic
of Philadelphia®

Dear Nobody,

Geoff visited me in the hospital today. I looked at him as if it were the first time I had ever seen him—though I knew it'd be the last. It was raining, but we still went for a walk. The cold was crisp and refreshing to my body; it caused a bearable pain in my joints that reminded me to be grateful that they still even work. Geoff was walking next to me—absentmindedly and aloof. Maybe that's the reason I love him; he always seems so distant, so dreamy. I never ask what it is he's got on his mind—instead I try to imagine it in my own. Undiscovered planets? Mystical worlds? Me being gone? It doesn't bother me that these worlds of his sometimes take him away from me for a while—I just hope that eventually he takes me with him.

We walked outside on the grounds around the hospital and then I had to go back in again. Back to the hell that had been so wrongly apportioned me. I asked him to come inside and sit with me for a while—while I got my treatment. I pleaded. But he said no.

I laughed the first time I heard I him say that he couldn't bear hospitals—just like everyone else he doesn't know what the word hospital really means.

In the hospital, we wear our IV scabs and scars like they are badges of bravery. We flaunt our paleness as one would

Children's Clinic
of Philadelphia®

flaunt beauty. In the hospital, each coughing fit is like a dutiful performance by the orchestra of viruses in our lungs—and we are obligated to do encores. Our frailness and weakness are signs of beauty—and suffering. In the hospital the machines and IV poles that you wheel along are like the status symbols the popular girls in high school wear around their necks.

In the hospital—the closer to death you are—the closer you are to sainthood.

☆

Children's Clinic
of Philadelphia®

Dear Nobody,

Geoff called me tonight and broke up with me. He said he couldn't take it.

I hate him.

I want to find the sharpest, biggest knife and stab him in the face.

☆

Dear Nobody,

Love is the creator of hate and the daughter of disappoint-
ment, as no two people could hurt each other more than two
people in love. Don't put too much LOVE into love. Love is
a whore to poets, musicians, songwriters, and artists; they use it
as fodder to sell their frustrations and personal impotence—and
love is TOO BIG a responsibility. No human can live up to
the capacity of love's expectations. A person will build you
up so high, but once you are elevated, it's all the harder when
you both fall. You become something to that person which is
impossible to live up to. Love has power, not the lovers.

Children's Clinic
of Philadelphia®

Dear Nobody,

Oh well, Geoff was a great distraction—while it lasted.

☆

Children's Clinic
of **Philadelphia**®

Dear Geoff,

Very late at night, when I can't sleep, and feel kind of lonely, I think of you. I remember about you, what you look like, what you feel and sound like. I remember interludes when we were together—and then it happens—I start to miss you in a painful way, and then I want for you to be mine again.

Then I soon realize that you are mine. I have you, trapped in my mind, until I decide to forget you. In my mind, I can see you whenever I want, staring or smiling at me. In my mind, I can make you laugh whenever I want, simply by recalling times that you did when we were together. I can feel the care and concern you showed me once, at a time I thought could never end; just by remembering.

If memories are all I'll have, I will still be thankful. In my memories I can distort you, and change or filter you to my perfection. Your touch is absent, but in my mind I can feel you everywhere, all around me. I close my eyes, enjoying the dark solitude, wishing that hope can be enough to force a memory of me to your mind.

Are you lonely? Am I in your dreams and constant thoughts? Do you hear a song—a sad one—and think of me?

I've got you trapped in my mind, but I know you are really gone.

Children's Clinic
of **Philadelphia®**

But for now, I think I'll just hold this key in my hand, and only let you out every once in a while, and as long as my memories are vibrant, you are always mine.

Love forever,
XOXOXOXO

Mary Rose

Dear Nobody,

I hate it in the hospital. I don't have any dignity in here—AT ALL. People just walk into my room whenever they want to. Shit, I'm lucky if they KNOCK. Nurses tell me to piss in a bowl, so they can save it for the doctors—or they tell me to shit in a bowl. Doctors stick their hands up my shirt. They ask me about my period—and if I'm sexually active. They tell me what and when to eat. They tell me to take deep breaths and give me fresh needles. Thank God I go home soon.

☆

Children's Clinic
of Philadelphia®

Dear Geoff,

you're a loser and a dickhead fag asshole.
    There is no life after Mary Rose.
    you'll be sorry babe.
    Goodbye.

Children's Clinic
of Philadelphia®

Dear Nobody,

I get out of the hospital tomorrow! Weeeee! I'm gonna take care of myself this time. No more drugs, no more drinking. I'm gonna make sure I never have to come back into this hell-hole ever again. I have a new perspective. I want to make real friends, have a real boyfriend and start over. I want to be well enough that I can start taking dance classes again and maybe move to New York. I want to become a famous dancer and get a rich boyfriend with a loft apartment and a white dog.

I think I can REALLY DO IT this time!

🖋

PHOENIXVILLE, PA
WINTER, 1999

Dear Nobody,

Wow! Three days out of the hospital and I'm already in love. His name is Jamie and he is absolutely perfect for me! Just one kiss from him got me higher than any bag of dope! (Cheaper, too). We met at the mall yesterday and he asked me for a cigarette. I said I didn't have one and he said that was cool, like he thought I wasn't putting on a front or something. We hung out all day. I shoplifted a CD from the Virgin store and gave it to him. I think that really impressed him. And then we went to the movies. Before my mom came to pick me up, he kissed me and asked for my number.

I really like him! I care about him a lot too. He's friendly, outgoing and physically he's so beautiful. I just knew it'd happen if I were patient—if I wanted it badly enough. I knew I'd meet my perfect guy. He's very sweet, but like most boys, a tad elusive. I haven't liked a guy this much for a very long time. I mean, he's not exactly poetry material (not yet, anyway) but I feel good about myself when I'm around him.

I met his friends yesterday and they are all older than I am. So I played the naïve youngster around them—partly to be taken under their wing and partly to be babied—and partly because I really DO need them to explain or direct me in some matters.

This girl I met a while ago knows him. They dated once—like a million years ago. She mentioned that he was a good guy, and that when they dated, he treated her like gold. I trust her, and I trust him, and my intuitions are rarely wrong (at least when my emotions are involved). I hope he understands that I wish only to offer him a pure "like" (not love, not now, it's WAY too soon). I told him that I've got a huge crush on him, and he said the same about me. Gosh, I like him so much; it kind of surprises me. Oh, he's so cute! I want to take things slowly because I want this to work out.

I think that there could be some major potential here. As long as I remember my social graces, and keep up my end of our relationships blueprints, things should be okay.

Man, I'm crushing on him so hard—and I love every minute of it! And that's the way a meaningful relationship should be!

☆

Dear Nobody,

Okay, now this guy Jamie is starting to tell me that he really likes me, that I'm different, and that he "cares" about me. I guess I really like him too, but I know how feelings can be—especially with guys—so I'm trying to distinguish the difference between his real feelings and his charm. I just really like him, and I want to believe him, but my self-protectiveness is admonishing me every time I want to gush over him in admiration. Maybe he does really feel this way? I don't want to be stupid and go ruining this by not believing him, or worrying too much if he's for real.

But what if he's really NOT for real?

Oh, to be sure. These things take time.

⭐

Children's Clinic
of **Philadelphia®**

Dear Nobody,

I had to cancel my date with Jamie today because I got sick again. Will this world ever give me a break? I'm taking care of myself okay—I've met a boy I like and I have a few good friends. Why can't this last awhile? Why can't God let me have my cake and eat it too—instead of always holding everything at arms length? I just have to be honest with myself. I will never be the happy, healthy girl with the nice boyfriend and the perfect home. It's not in the cards for me.

This is my reality: this morning—just like so many other mornings—I awake to the bitter veneration of nauseating medicine as the taste of a "treatment" fills my mouth and lungs. A loud angry machine squeezes my chest as it pounds, pushes and vibrates my lungs—every morning of every day, only minutes after I wake up.

This is my reality: I live in hospitals, not homes. My own body, the temple of my soul, is my worst enemy. I live within it every painful moment of my life. I am held captive by its destructive viruses, deteriorating bacteria, and excruciating disease.

This is my reality: Vicious day in, and vicious day out, this is my fate. Coughing up blood from my lungs while I choke on sticky, painful plugs of fatal bacteria-infected mucus.

Children's Clinic
of Philadelphia®

Every day of my depraved life, I am chastised for being still half-alive.

<u>That is my reality.</u>

☆

Children's Clinic
of Philadelphia®

Dear Nobody,

After I'm in the hospital for a while I start to feel really ugly. I mean, I know when you're sick you're not supposed to be like all alluring with oxygen prongs in your nose and tangled hair that you're too sick to brush and a swollen face from steroids— but still.

Know how on talk shows and shit all those psychiatrists talk about how adolescent girls feel self-conscious because they're not used to all the changes their bodies are going through yet? I guess I feel like that with my weight. When I'm not sick, I usually weigh 108 pounds, and when I'm sick around 97. Right now I weigh 101. It's hard to imagine 108 as my normal weight after spending weeks inside my 97 pound body. And after a while of being 108, it's hard to imagine myself as 97. My weight just changes so much so fast. When I had the temporary diabetes I lost almost ten pounds in eight days, and once I gained seven pounds overnight. Now, I'm supposed to have my weight up as high as I can and eat as much as I can.

I don't know, it's weird not having a definite body size or shape. I like to wear dresses, but when I buy a dress it may be too small or too big a week later. I usually end up buying non-fitted skirts, because they're easier to wear with different sizes than dresses—even though one day they will just fit, then

Children's Clinic
of **Philadelphia®**

the next month go down to my knees or calves.
But that probably bothers me the least of anything...

☆

Children's Clinic
of Philadelphia®

Dear Nobody,

I'm getting out of the hospital today. They told me if I continue drinking and doing drugs I would cut my life expectancy in half. The doctor told me that if I preserve myself long enough I'd live to be thirty five—maybe even forty. I could even stay healthy until a cure is found; which everyone says is going to be really soon. But I've been hearing that since I was seven years old.

And guess what?

I'm losing patience.

The doctor put me on bed rest for three days and upped my medication. I'm not getting much better, but my condition has stabilized. I don't care either way; I just want to be home.

☆

Dear Nobody,

I'm getting kind of old now. I'm not ready to be eighteen. I'm not even ready for seventeen or sixteen. I don't feel or seem any older than fifteen. Maybe they're other reasons for it, but I don't know. I feel like I've always had to grow up so much faster than I wanted to. I held on to childhood as long as I could. Maybe adolescence will be the same. Could that be dangerous to me—counterproductive?

I don't know. Who can say about the future?

Who cares?

All I want is security. I just need to be sure that I'll be okay.

I think it must be this town. I hate it. That's not a good attitude to have, but it's true. Besides, it COULD MAYBE be dangerous to like such a shitty town. I'd have to lower my standard of happiness to be happy around here.

I guess I've really got no place else to go. So I leave mentally. I'm becoming a pretty good dreamer—a shiftless lay about. It's really not so bad. There's lots of freedom—even if freedom is just another word for nothing left to lose. I've got peace—and that's what I need right now—(besides sleep)—so GOODNIGHT!

☆

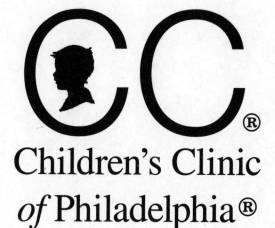

Children's Clinic
of Philadelphia®

WINTER, 1999

CC.
Children's Clinic
of Philadelphia®

Dear Nobody,

I knew long before it happened—that I would have to go into the hospital again. I had been sick for weeks and I wasn't getting any better—I was just getting worse and worse. I could really feel it this time; it took so much energy to even sit up. If I took a shower, I'd have to sit down to catch my breath. Everything I did reminded me that I was dying. Piles of tissues filled with green-brown bloody mucus covered my bed and the floor by the couch. In my room, if I couldn't find any tissues or clothing to use—I would just spit it out on the floor. My mom thought it was really disgusting, but I didn't care. When you wake up at four in the morning choking on horrible tasting shit, I don't care where it goes as long as it's out of my body.

This most recent hospitalization was one of the most painful episodes. I thought I was going to die this time—I was sure of it. It will be the sixth time this year that I've had to be admitted. My mother and I drove to Philly in silence.

After being admitted, I tried to fall asleep—even though I wasn't sure if I'd ever wake up. I wanted my mother to be aware of what was happening but I also just wanted to be alone. It was weird—I wasn't scared at all. Even though I was in pain and exhausted, I felt like, I don't know—content?

I just lay there, waiting. I didn't pray to live or die. I didn't

try to barter with God the way I usually do, promising to stop using drugs and abusing my body. I knew it wouldn't work—and I didn't want to die a liar. I was really just praying to thank God and everyone for the life I'd had.

I turned on the Religion Channel and listened to a group of people praying. I couldn't talk, but I said the prayers in my head, mostly Hail Mary's and the Our Father prayer. I tried to whisper the bedtime prayer I used to say to myself when I was little: "Now I lay me down to sleep, I pray the Lord my Soul to keep, and if I die before I wake, I pray the lord my soul to take."

It felt like someone else was in the room with me then—more than the machines beeping and oxygen hissing—I just felt like other people were there. I thought of the other people I knew with Cystic Fibrosis and prayed some more. Now I know how they felt when they were dying...

☆

CC.
Children's Clinic
of Philadelphia®

Dear Nobody,

You can learn a lot about life while being surrounded by death. I'm kept up almost every night by my roommate's excruciating screams of pain. Some of these children's screams can wake you from a deep sleep—but others, like my roommate—have enough vigor inside them to put the fear of God into you. Maybe it's just knowing how it feels to be the one screaming, and then having to listen to someone else being put through the same thing? It's not that I'm scared she is dying. I know that when you're in the very WORST pain, you can't even scream out.

Earlier today when I was asleep—nodding out from the morphine—my roommate went into convulsions. I woke up from the sound of her bed shaking and rang for the nurse. Later that day, my roommate's mom came in to visit her and brought her younger brother and sister. They looked about eight or nine years old. They were sitting around her bed talking. I saw her lean forward to grab something, when suddenly she shot straight up into the air and her eyes rolled back. Her tongue was sticking out and wagging from side to side. One rail on the side of her bed was up, and I thought she'd bump her head on it or something.

Her mom started to scream, "No! No! Taha! Taha! My

Children's Clinic
of Philadelphia®

baby! No! Not again! It's too much for my baby!" Then she yelled for her son to go get the nurse. He stood gaping and wide eyed—as I must have been. Her mom started screaming again and flew on top of the bed, trying to restrain the girl's head. I grabbed my bell and called the nurse. A bunch of nurses came running in all at once and rolled down the head of the bed—then put the rails up. They wheeled her out of the room very quickly and her family followed. <u>I haven't seen her since.</u>

I can't say it's ever dull around here.

Children's Clinic
of Philadelphia®

Dear Nobody,

A friend of mine from the hospital came to visit me today. She's one of those "miracle" cases. One of those few people I know who took care of herself and is in an almost perfect, healthy condition, despite having been born with Cystic Fibrosis. When I first met her she was sicker than I was. She was eighteen and they had given her seven months to live. Now its five years later and she's perfectly healthy.

Seeing her for the first time in so many years was amazing. Without even speaking, she managed to convince me of her dignity. She had an awe-inspiring strength. After seeing so much tragedy, after bearing such pains, and facing the dread of such mournful losses—her strength was still there. Her intoxicating smile, even if only halfhearted, reflected such radiance and spirit. Unlike other people who had seen only half of such tragedies, she had not become ravaged and haggard from life. Instead, her suffering seemed to proclaim her will, strength and vibrancy. I feel like she is a hundred times better than any other human being I know. Even though she is fairly young, she is as mature as many sages. Even though her beauty is not much a cosmetic, physical one, she is always the most attractive person in the room.

She inspired me to stop drinking and try to take care of

Children's Clinic
of Philadelphia®

myself. I want to live to see twenty-three, like she has. I want to look beautiful and wise and strong. I want to visit people I had known from my time in the hospital—people who were worse off than me—and tell them that it was going to all be okay. That we could fight this.

That I was fighting it—and I was winning.

☆

Children's Clinic
of Philadelphia®

Dear Nobody,

At night, when most of the patients are asleep, me and some of the other sick kids all congregate and sneak through the halls together. We have to push our beeping IV poles in front of us or roll around in broken child-size wheelchairs—but at least it's quiet and we can talk. Sometimes we talk for hours—all night. We talk of how most of the people that used to visit us don't anymore, just because it had gotten so common to hear that we were in the hospital again.

I remember once when I was in the hospital for fourteen days and only my mother came to see me. Yet for the duration I was in the hospital, my cousin had broken her leg. So while I was dying in a hospital with chronic disease, she was the one being comforted by our family members. They were not coming to see me, but they were bringing her flowers, balloons, cards. After a while, I guess, people just don't want to deal with you anymore. They don't want to see you getting sicker; taking more medicine than grandma does. After a while, people don't even call to ask how you are—because they don't want to hear that your sputum tested positive for blood—or that you've lost more weight. Yes, after a while— those cards and flowers and phone calls fade away, much like your health. And the other lonely, sickly freaks become your

Children's Clinic
of Philadelphia®

new family because to the rest of the healthy people we know, we have already died.

It's haunting to think that my family members will not drive an hour to come and visit me while I am in the hospital and yet I know they would drive two hours to attend my funeral.

Me and the other kids here talk about death a lot. I remember the last time I was here, Jennifer was asking me what I heard it felt like to die with CF? Jennifer learned how before I did. She died here.

We talked about how it felt to be mocked because of our coughing—how being made fun of could hurt more than the actual pain of coughing.

One girl I know told me about how when she was diagnosed, her mother dropped her off at her father's house—and never came back. She told me how much she had cried and how she had held a gun to her head, ready to kill herself. I asked her why she never did it. She stared at the tubes in her arm—made fists out of her fingers and looked straight into my eyes—but never answered me. She knew I already knew the answer. We all felt that way before. We've felt enough despair, enough guilt—even just physical pain. So many reasons to do it. But we aren't built that way. We've become machines. We're used to the pain.

Needles in our arms, tubes running through our noses and

Children's Clinic
of Philadelphia®

chests, equipment shoved in our mouth or down our throat. Probing examinations and embarrassing questions. Terrible loneliness day in and day out. If that didn't kill us, maybe nothing could.But the one thing I noticed we never talked about was our future. I don't think we saw much of a future for ourselves. Besides, what use was there talking about the future? We all knew what the future meant for us.

And it starts with a D.

Children's Clinic
of Philadelphia®

Dear Nobody,

Every night I am on a breathing monitor. Tonight, after I fell asleep, I unconsciously ripped out those prongs and the fucking monitor started screaming—BEEP, BEEP, BEEP—that constant wail waking me up. This happens ALL the time and the nurses have to run in and fix the oxygen setup. Tonight, this one ugly fat nurse threatened to tape the tubes to my face if I ripped them off again.

★

Children's Clinic
of **Philadelphia®**

Dear Nobody,

Tell me, does everyone feel like I do?

Oh God, please help me, please.

No one on my floor cares for me. No one loves as I do, or feels as I do. I try not to feel, but my humanity will not let me.

Kill this hurt of mine Jesus.

Please. Oh, how can I keep on like this?

None of you bastards will know the half of it. EVER. No one else could bear the entirety of my hell-born situation.

What else could there be left for me?

Tell me.

No, don't.

Who knows what I know, who's been where I have? I've never imagined, even in my most dreaded nightmares, that I would become this.

Oh God, please help me. Help me. I need your help. I simply cannot attain this life. I've tried. I've tried so hard.

Oh God, please cure me soon.

I hurt, I hurt. I hurt so bad.

Humans could never know.

Oh, help me please now, please.

All I ever did was love you…

✡

Children's Clinic
of Philadelphia®

Dear Nobody,

Have I had a revelation, or a breakdown? I feel completely detached lately, from everyone. I don't feel isolated. I just feel like I don't need them. I feel more peaceful when people aren't around. I want to be the only person in the room when I die, and I want it to be dark outside.

Children's Clinic
of Philadelphia®

Dear Nobody,

I woke up coughing around three in the morning. After I stopped coughing, it just got worse. I couldn't breathe. I had these nasty, sharp pains all through my lungs. The nurse called in three resident doctors and a respiratory therapist. I got a treatment and some of the pain left but then five minutes later I got worse. I felt so exhausted; all I could do was try and breathe. Sitting up for the doctors felt impossible. They gave me oxygen and told me to stay calm. I felt like the shit in my lungs was turning into cement—like I was being stabbed in the chest.

Even though the pain was worse than before, I lied and told the doctors I felt much better. I didn't want them to be in the room if this was it…

☆

Touched by a rose so red...
Soon to make us dead...
Touched by a rose so red...
Dying in our rose-bed...
65 roses, Cystic fibrosis...

Mary Rose died from complications caused by cystic fibrosis on February 12, 1999.

Dear Nobody,

I guess I like to be alone and relax in solitude, but I also love huge crowds of people. Someday I want crowds to come to see me, en masse, just to watch me. Sing, act, speak, whatever, I don't care, as long as it's all for me.

I want to be so rich that I could donate millions to different charities—and still be FILTHY RICH. I want diamonds, gold, silver, rings, bracelets, and tons of necklaces and earrings. I want to see my reflection from an extravagant dressing room vanity decorated with satin, lace, feathers and bright lights that make my skin glow. Gowns with sequins and lace, rhinestones and silk, and only the best patent leather shoes (with heels) will be all I ever wear in public (unless of course one of my character roles call for something else) and my roles of course will only be starring ones, and none of my understudies will be as talented or beautiful or loved (unless they are full of MY characteristics). Jacuzzis, spas, heated kidney-bean-shaped swimming pools, and extravagant bubble baths in gigantic bathrooms will be my leisure hangouts (WHEN I'm not signing autographs, or visiting children's hospitals, or at book signings).

My death would bring melancholy to nations all over, and they will mourn my loss with such honor and respect that I'll never be forgotten.

I can dream, can't I?

Love, Mary Rose XOXO

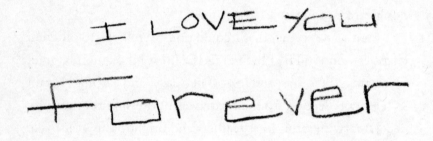

THE END

☆

Afterword

When Gillian and Legs first told me that they loved Mary Rose through her journals and wanted to take on the project of having them published, I could hardly believe it. I mean, what were the chances that two talented and experienced authors would happen upon these journals—and love them—and want to see them published? Here were the authors of one of Mary Rose's favorite books that she owned, *Please Kill Me: The Uncensored Oral History of Punk* interested in collaborating with her.

To consider that Mary Rose's thoughts, words, stories would be out there to be shared with so many other people was overwhelming. I knew, as did everyone else who knew Mary Rose, what an incredibly amazing person she was. Now, through this book, all those who come to know her will keep her in their hearts—her wild humor, her gifted imagination, her excruciating pain, and her heroic strength. This is her new beginning.

As with most new beginnings there were obstacles. Making the decision to share Mary Rose's journals was the first one. Would Mary Rose want her thoughts and feelings shared with others, especially people who didn't know her? I wrestled with this and also asked a few of her friends and family for their opinion. Consensus was, although not unanimously, that since Mary Rose loved writing, storytelling, and dreamed of being an author someday, she would want this. Most believe, including me, that she even had some involvement in helping with connections that made this book happen. So with that being decided, her dream of being a published author will be fulfilled. Those of us who love her hope that her story will help other young people who may be experiencing seemingly insurmountable struggles of their own.

There were also legal obstacles. The law required signatures from both Mary Rose's parents to get copyrights for her journals. It took months and significant expense to locate Mary Rose's father, and when he finally was contacted he was indifferent and uncooperative. His main concern was what she may have written about him. He was assured there would be nothing. It seemed that after having very little involvement with her in life, he now wanted to control what was left. Gillian, Legs, and I persevered through this process, and after lengthy and discouraging setbacks we were able to move forward with the copyrights. Again, if not for Gillian and Legs' support, this would not have been possible.

Finally here it is. The book completed. Although I am not proud of some of my life choices when I was younger, I could not be any more proud of Mary Rose. Her sister and I miss her every day and love her deeply. Although Mary Rose often wrote to express feeling lonely, angry, betrayed by others or her own body, Mary Rose knew she was loved. I know she didn't focus her writing on positive things or happy occasions in her life and at times she exaggerated the negative. That's OK. Her writing helped her through the darker times and I'm immensely grateful she found some solace with that.

A special thank you to the Geller family, especially Lauren, for introducing Mary Rose's journals to Legs and Gillian. If not for your interest and enthusiasm for her writing, her journals most likely would still be in the bedroom closet where you and Leanne first saw them and started to read.

I want to express my overwhelming gratitude to Gillian McCain and Legs McNeil for taking the time to read the journals of a girl you didn't know who was writing to nobody. I could not be happier that you felt and appreciated the life force of Mary Rose through her journals and that you took the time and energy to do something extraordinary for her. Also your kindness and sensitivity towards me has been astounding and you will always have a special place in my mind and heart.

To Mary Rose—my little rose bud—

I LOVE YOU LOVE YOU LOVE YOU

Forever and Always

MOM

Acknowledgments

We would like to thank Jonathon Marder for giving our manuscript to Joni Evans, who in turn gave it to Kirby Kim, who sold it to Sourcebooks. We are grateful to all of you.

Also to Fred and Regina and their daughter Lauren—this book couldn't have happened without you guys.

For design, scanning, copyediting, and inscribing we like to thank Kristina Berg, Tom Hearn, Ryan Adie, Keoin Nostadt, and Megan Cump.

And all of our lawyers: for early legal advice, Rick Rheinhold; for contract advice, Eric Brown. And for fighting through the trenches with great patience, Keith McWhirk. Keith, we couldn't have done this without you.

For a supportive shoulder and an eager ear, James Marshall.

To the Sourcebooks team: Todd, Leah, Cat, and anyone else who touched this book.

For all of our early readers who encouraged us not to give up: Ann Evans, Tom and Ann Hearn, Amy Haben, Joanne Sorenson, Rebecca Vasquez, Bob and Elizabeth Gruen, Mike DeCapite, Matt Muhall and Ami Dushkowitch, Eric Swenson,

Jo Ann Wasserman, Janice Johnson, Diana Rickard, Barb DeLong, and for any names we missed, please forgive us.

To the H.H. McCain family for always being there for us.

But mostly, to Mary Rose's mother and sister, for putting their trust in us.

LONG LIVE, MARY ROSE!

About the Authors

Gillian McCain and Legs McNeil are the co-authors of *Please Kill Me: The Uncensored Oral History of Punk*. When they aren't collaborating, McCain writes poetry and McNeil writes non-fiction. They are currently working on two new oral histories together.